W9-BSZ-733

EDUCATIONAL CHANGE:
The Reality and the Promise

A Report on the National Seminars on Innovation,
Honolulu, July 2-23, 1967

Edited by Richard R. Goulet

Chief, Program Dissemination
Division of Plans and Supplementary Centers
U.S. Office of Education

The National Seminars on Innovation were sponsored by the Institute
for the Development of Educational Activities (/I/D/E/A/), a
division of the Charles F. Kettering Foundation, Dayton, Ohio, in
cooperation with the U.S. Office of Education.

Citation Press, New York · 1968

Library of Congress Catalog Card Number: 68-27152

Cover design by June Martin.

1st printing June 1968
Printed in the U.S.A.

Communication of ideas is essential to real improvement in any field of endeavor. In the field of education, such sharing of ideas is vital, for education is at a crucial, transitional point today. Education is being called upon to solve many more of the complex problems confronting our society. At the same time, educators are realizing that drastic changes in educational methods and techniques are necessary to aid in solving today's problems, as well as to attain traditional educational aims.

Current local, state, and national efforts to solve these problems have been exciting and innovative. To be truly effective and widespread, however, such endeavors and ideas must be assessed and communicated. To this important aim, the National Seminars on Innovation were directed. In the seminars educators shared and debated their ideas in an effort to better focus efforts to improve elementary and secondary education.

How can federal, state, and local monies be spent most effectively to allow each human being to develop to his optimum capacity? This was the underlying theme of the many different ideas explored during the seminars. But the goal of human development through education has many facets demanding a variety of approaches. How can we help disadvantaged and minority group children? How can we improve educational programs for young children? How can we provide educational excellence for children in geographically isolated areas? How can each child be enabled to learn at his own best pace? Answering these questions demands new attitudes and innovative techniques and methods.

To share and develop solutions to these problems is of great concern to our nation and all its people. These seminars of sharing, thus, have made a vital contribution to American education through meaningful communication that will, hopefully, spread throughout the nation.

NOLAN ESTES, Associate Commissioner
Elementary and Secondary Education
U. S. Office of Education

Contents

Into the Future with Our Changing Schools

Education and Societal Needs

Systematic and Effective Innovation

Creative Directions for Innovation by Governments, Universities, and Industry

State of Technology in Education and Its Further Development and Implementation

Preface

THE NATIONAL SEMINARS on Innovation boldly voiced our national commitment to promote creative change in educational practices. The nearly 1,000 educators who actively participated in the seminars' activities analyzed the elements required for effective change as well as the efforts being made by various sectors to bring about change.

Presentations by leading figures from American industry, government, and education, coupled with working exhibits of important advances in education technology, not only gave participants new insights but aroused constructive debate.

The seminars underscored the fact that new educational concepts and technology are merely the promise for educational change, not the reality. To impose these upon our schools without proper software or program development is to cast them into oblivion. All innovations can become trivialities when a teacher closes the classroom door. Therefore, to be effective, change must be planned. Innovations should be understood, teachers should be trained and made receptive to new ideas, and new devices should be tested and evaluated before new programs can be adapted meaningfully.

This report presents an abundance of ideas. Some are illuminating, others controversial, still others generally accepted; but all are important concepts concerning the goals and requirements for better education.

The National Seminars on Innovation provided a vital force

for generating a dialogue among American educators aimed at identifying and adapting the new ideas, hardware, and software continuously advanced by government, industry, universities, and public school systems.

SAMUEL G. SAVA
Executive Director
Institute for Development of
    Educational Activities

Introduction

THE PRESENT EMPHASIS upon innovative educational change must be viewed and understood within its larger societal context. If schools have been functioning in a vacuum, then it is time to change the system, revamp our thinking, and search for bold new methods to provide our nation's children with the highest quality of education.

This was the fundamental message that echoed throughout the three National Seminars on Innovation, held in Honolulu from July 2 to July 23, 1967. The seminars were sponsored jointly by the U. S. Office of Education through its nationwide program for educational innovation, PACE (Projects to Advance Creativity in Education), funded under Title III of the Elementary and Secondary Education Act, and by the Charles F. Kettering Foundation through its action-oriented educational innovation division, /I/D/E/A/ (Institute for the Development of Educational Activities). Codirectors of the seminars were Norman E. Hearn, Chief of the Program Development and Dissemination Branch, U. S. Office of Education, and B. Frank Brown, Director of Information and Services, /I/D/E/A/. Herbert W. Wey, Associate Dean of the College of Education, University of Miami, was general chairman of seminar activities.

Nearly 1,000 educators from throughout the United States participated in a program designed to improve elementary and secondary education by: expanding knowledge of existing research, theory, and practical application in education and related fields; providing training in the technical aspects of program management; and broadening working relationships between local, state, and federal officials and between theorists and practicing educators.

Each six-day seminar program was attended by about 135 elementary and secondary school administrators and 165 directors of outstanding PACE projects. Many of the participants were /I/D/E/A/ Fellows, school administrators selected by the Kettering Foundation as potential leaders for American educational improvement.

The seminars were conducted in an exciting, newly constructed building on the campus of The Kamehameha Schools. The building was an innovation in itself. Its hexagonal rooms provided a natural setting for the seminars, and its versatile communications facilities — from telephone to loudspeaker public address system to closed-circuit television — enabled seminar participants to interact most advantageously in large and small group sessions.

The entire proceedings of the National Seminars on Innovation were video taped through the courtesy of the Ampex Corporation. Video tapes of individual presentations as well as a highlights tape of the overall conference are available for closed-circuit use. These Ampex tapes are being distributed without cost by the Institute for Development of Educational Activities, P. O. Box 446, Melbourne, Florida 32901.

All the events of the seminar are not reported here, nor does the order of the contents of this publication follow the organization of the seminars themselves. This report is divided into five parts, which reflect the most crucial educational concerns confronting society today. These concerns were examined by seminar participants through discussions and interaction with national authorities in such fields as curriculum development, sociology, psychology, technology, and learning theory. As a result, some illuminating answers are presented to the following questions:

How can we design programs to make education more relevant to the needs of today's children who are often confused about their roles in society or unsure of their personal values?

How can teacher roles and attitudes be changed, and what methods might be developed for the selection and training of school personnel?

What so-called innovations are or are not working and why?

How can schools innovate systematically and effectively?

What direction for creative educational change now is given, or should be given, by universities, private foundations, industry, and state and federal governments?

What is the state and effectiveness of technology in education, and what are the roles of educators and representatives of industry in its further development and implementation?

Each section in the report is preceded by overviews highlighting the individual presentations. A summary of ideas for educational innovation, compiled from recommendations made by small interaction groups that met regularly during the seminars, is included as an appendix.

The editor assumes full responsibility for errors in interpretation that may have resulted from restructuring and excluding certain materials from the contributions to this report.

RICHARD R. GOULET
Editor

Into the Future with Our Changing Schools

Overviews

EDUCATIONAL CHANGE: VALUES AND GOALS

John I. Goodlad

Preoccupation with the status quo and educational trivialities must end. Modern educators must concentrate on
changing rigid, traditional educational standards such as
conventional school building design, standard school entrance age, the 6-3-3 school structure plan, standard school
hours, the nine-month school year, a balance of subjects, and
grade levels.

In eliminating these hindrances to the education of the
child in a technology-oriented society, educators must become concerned with the fulfillment of five major goals: enabling the child to acquire a meaningful grasp of his culture,
developing a real relationship between education and basic
human values, dealing effectively with individual differences
in children, enabling children to develop a sense of personal
identity that will help overcome the ever-growing problems of
alienation, and developing the role of education in the process of increasing intervention in human evolution.

For meaningful attainment, however, these goals must be

considered in relation to the primary question, which is not "what knowledge is of most worth?" but "what kinds of human beings do we want to produce?"

INNOVATION AND TEACHER ROLES

J. Lloyd Trump

Teachers aren't conditioning themselves for the new educational climate; they must adopt new roles to accommodate new trends and innovative practices in the attainment of three crucially important educational goals: individualizing pupil learning, professionalizing teaching, and refining curriculum content.

To individualize pupil learning, teachers must give students more opportunities for independent study and must provide for students' continuous progress and individual evaluation through the identification of instructional goals that are defined in terms of changed human behavior.

To professionalize teaching, administrators must utilize individual differences in teachers and must also schedule teachers with pupil groups for not more than half the school day. Teachers must utilize technical devices effectively and must change their attitude toward the use of auxiliary personnel from "I know what is best for my class" to "Someone else can do certain tasks better."

To refine curriculum content, required learnings must be defined and creative and depth studies stimulated.

TEACHER TRAINING AND SELECTION

Donald N. Bigelow

The transactions that take place between the teacher and the student constitute the most important element requiring change in American education today. Therefore, the primary need for our schools is better teachers. But four red herrings are obscuring our vision in the development of good teachers: the present preoccupation with innovation, curriculum development, educational technology, and scholarship.

School administrators have the responsibility to direct attention away from these red herrings, which are merely educational substitutes for good teachers. At present our universities are stressing the acquisition of knowledge at the expense of training people how to teach. As the greatest consumer of the universities' output, school administrators can demand superior preparation of teachers. They must look to the universities and prescribe standards of quality, declining to accept those teachers who fail to meet their specifications.

THE SUBORDINATION OF TEACHING TO LEARNING
Caleb Gattegno

Subordinating teaching to learning is essential if American education is to improve substantially. Before this approach can be utilized, two basic misconceptions about learning that underlie the present system of education must be eliminated: that one learns by imitation and that one retains learning through memory. We do not learn primarily by imitation. We all have extraordinary mental powers that we know how to use discriminately from birth; we use them, for example, in learning to talk, and we retain learning through functioning, as when we acquire the skill of driving.

These truths must underlie the process of formal education, in a subordination of teaching to learning. Using this approach, students are taught to remember as little as possible; instead, criteria are developed in their minds that help them acquire a progressively greater degree of discrimination and independence. They know and understand how to generate answers, one from another, via controlled transformations.

Applying this approach to learning how to read, for example, results in the mastery of the techniques of reading in a matter of hours — sometimes less than ten.

THE HUMANITIES IN TRANSITION

Harry L. Levy

The humanities need help if they are to survive in this period of transition when they are competing with the sciences for students' attention. Computer technology may provide some aid in two problem areas confronting the study of the humanities: the absorption of peripheral facts and the use of the English language.

Although nothing about the intrinsic meaning and value of a literary masterpiece can or should be programed, the peripheral facts about authors and masterpieces can be reduced to a computer program that a student can learn in his own time, at his own pace. Then the teacher is free to stimulate and respond to the student's thoughts about the important intrinsic worth of the literary work and its relevance today.

To study the humanities, students must also be able to communicate at the formal level of English, and this presents another problem that can be alleviated through modern educational methods. Many students who function well in every day communication do not function well in formal communication. To correct this situation, pattern–practice, based upon structural linguistic analysis, should be employed to teach English as though it were a foreign language, or at least a second language.

SCHOOLHOUSE IN TRANSITION

Harold B. Gores

At last the walls are coming down, and the self-contained, self-contaminating classroom is giving way to open space that children and teachers can arrange to suit their needs. Innovative school building design should look to nature for function, beauty, and economy. Classroom space might be likened to a great pond on which the ducks (teachers) and ducklings (children) swim about during the day. The ideal classroom would have sail-like partitions, moored against the bank, that could be floated across the pond to constitute classrooms as required. The sails might be multicolored and puffed with kangaroo pouches for storage. Such a flexible and malleable environment would enable teachers to reconstitute instant classrooms by "sailing" walls up whenever visual privacy was needed.

This is one example of present innovative school construction, which is moving away from the old puritan notion of austerity. Children are winning a new right — the right to be comfortable, which means that the reverberative, ceramic, masonry box that is the classroom is being softened. Comfort can make as much as a 15 per cent difference in the productivity of children and teachers.

Educational Change: Values and Goals

John I. Goodlad

To DISCUSS THE IDEA of the changing schools requires first a clarification: that is that all of us educators, however innovative we may be, are really preoccupied with problems of maintaining the status quo. The changes we make are peripheral. It is also true that there probably is no innovation ever created by man for education that has the power needed to bring about the evolution in our schools that all of us realize must take place continuously and in an accelerated fashion during the balance of this century.

One of the great challenges to each educational leader then is to surmount the barrier of educational trivialities in order to consider the major ideas and issues confronting us. Trivialities include such things as whether we should have report cards, parent conferences, and homework. Unfortunately, we have tended to involve our communities in dialogues over these kinds of issues. Thus, my plea is really that we raise the level of discourse about education, even as we continue to run our schools smoothly and efficiently by solving these trivial problems.

GOALS, PROBLEMS, AND ISSUES

In raising the level of discourse, there are five main goals with which we should be concerned. First, each child should acquire a meaningful grasp of his culture and develop the kinds of intellectual tools that will enable him to deal with it. Second, schools must have a real relationship to basic human values. Third, schools must learn to deal with individual differences. Fourth, we must develop a sense of personal identity to overcome our problems of alienation. And finally, we must consider the merging problems resulting from the possibilities of intervening in human evolution.

A Realistic Grasp of Culture

Stimulating youngsters to acquire a realistic grasp of their culture initially entails a quantitative problem. All of us are faced with the problem of the sheer mass of the accumulation of human knowledge. In the future we no longer can deal with this problem by designing a schedule called an education, in which the teacher plays the game of up-to-here by Halloween and up-to-here by Christmas and hopes to cover the work of the grade by the end of the year. This approach is a complete anachronism in face of the realities of the knowledge explosion.

In using this approach, we are not acknowledging the fact that knowledge is what one perceives. When I was a youngster in elementary school, it scarcely dawned on me that knowledge was anything other than immutable — something given to me, unchanging, fixed, and here. Studies of present teaching in elementary classrooms suggest that a very large percentage of our schools still appear committed to the notion that knowledge is immutable. Too few youngsters are grasping the notion that knowledge is indeed man-made and that they and other human beings produce it.

A child must realize that there are differing points of view, that an individual's position in relation to the world determines what he sees, and that research is merely a vehicle for inducing greater reliability and validity for observations of phenomena. Robert Corplus, one of the truly stimulating educators, conducts a science program for youngsters that begins with the notion of a Mr. O, who stands back and looks at things, and where he stands and the glasses he wears have a great deal to do with what he sees.

The curriculum reform movement of the past 15 years has attempted to bring order out of chaos in regard to the quantitative concept of knowledge and has also tried to help youngsters recognize that knowledge is what man perceives. There must be an intensification of this approach to the curriculum.

The curriculum must also be reduced to the utmost simplicity. Professor Benjamin S. Blum has pointed out that if a youngster is not learning an area of knowledge, it is probably because educators have not simplified it to the point where he can manage it. Too often we feel that a student is not bright enough, rather than reversing this attitude and asking, "How do we reduce these concepts to their utmost simplicity so that the student can work effectively with a quantitative problem?"

In other words, we must find ways of restructuring knowledge to make it manageable, and, generally, we must enable students to grasp the idea of individual perception and production of knowledge.

A Real Relationship Between Education and Human Values

We must also develop a real relationship between education and basic human values. Unfortunately, success in school predicts success in school; grades predict grades — not compassion, not good work habits, not vocational correlation, not social success, not marital success, not happiness, not any human virtue one could name. The correlation in every study made so far on this relationship has reached only .22 as the highest index, and a .22 correlation is completely worthless for any predictive purpose. At present there is no relationship between what is rewarded in school and the later practice of human virtue. One of the greatest challenges as we move into the future is to develop some meaningful relationship between the expectations of our schools and the expectations we have for human beings in later life.

To achieve such a relationship, we must first make education correspond to life. For example, we might schedule a program with busses going everywhere so that children can study directly. A school is physically only a box. We should break free of this box mentally, for it is shameful how little we use the educational resources that surround us everywhere.

Individual Differences

How little still do we cater to the individual differences of human beings, even though we are aware of those differences. There are numerous statistics that exist on the range of individual differences from trait to trait within a single human being, and these data demonstrate that the variation in one human being in regard to the various aspects of his learning is 80 per cent as variable as the variation within a group itself. This means that if a teacher is teaching the fifth grade and doing it well, he is teaching all the grades from second to eighth, since there are only 0 to 5 children in his class performing at fifth-grade level. In comparison with other important areas of education, we know a great deal about individual differences, but the gap is formidable between what we know and what we do about these differences.

Nongrading is one effective method of dealing with individual differences, and the notion of nongrading is now virtually accepted by educators in the United States. The UCLA elementary school reports a distinct shift in questions raised by its 5,000 visitors each year. Less than five years ago, visitors were suspicious and skeptical about the nongrading concept. They asked, "What is the evidence? Where is the research? What makes you think this is better than the plan that we have been using in the past?" Now most visitors ask, "How do you do it?"

Thus, we are in a process, and will be for some 15 years, of attempting to implement the innovations of the 1950's to refine what might well be called a human-based school. Research indicates that every major city in the United States today has seriously considered, or is seriously considering, the implementation of nongrading in some form. Interestingly enough, cities usually consider using nongrading in working with the disadvantaged child where, clearly, learning problems appear to be the most severe. If we believe that nongrading is effective for these children, it must have meaning for the others.

What lies in the future regarding individual differences? It probably is physically impossible for a teacher to deal with the total range of individual problems presented by each youngster; thus, the self-contained classroom will disappear as rapidly as we are capable of effecting new modes of learning. One new mode of learning that has already been effected is team teaching.

Concurrent with arranging teachers in teams, it is possible to utilize a vast variety of people with special talents, arranging them under horizontal coordinates who relate all parts of the program and under vertical coordinates who are responsible for the various areas of learning. Thus a subject-matter specialist can be used without departmentalization. There has never been an adequate set of arguments for either departmentalization or the self-contained classroom.

Modular scheduling is another approach to individualizing learning, but all these approaches, like nongrading and team teaching, are in a sense trivialities since our real aim is to find an educational program that deals with the unique differences of youngsters; these differences cannot be organized away, used away, or otherwise disposed of. Thus, the continuing problem of the educator is to create ways of dealing with differences.

Alienation and Loss of Identity

The educator also must concern himself with another facet of the nature of human beings that has evolved into a major problem of our culture — the sense of alienation and loss of identity that is, and will continue to be, so prevalent in our world. Partly attributable to this sense of alienation is the dropout problem, a problem not confined to the disadvantaged. R. Louis Bright, U.S. Associate Commissioner of Education for Research in Education, spoke recently about data gathered on the IQ's of dropouts. He was startled to find that some of these studies revealed an average IQ level of about 108. This is not surprising, for some of our most gifted college students are dropouts. The problem begins very early in our schools where youngsters drop out psychologically, if not physically. In some American schools the nonpromotion rate varies from 0 per cent to 50 per cent. Why? Is it merely that some youngsters are more stupid than others? No, the fact is that teachers differ in their values toward the promotion question. One important reason a youngster with an IQ of 110 and a certain learning rate failed in one school and a similar pupil in another school did not was that their teachers possessed different values.

However, even if this disparity in teachers' values did not exist, we would still have to contend with numerous physical and psychological dropouts, for this problem stems partially from the technological evolution that has been such a dominant feature of 20th-century life. Educators must cope with these technological advances and utilize them to improve the school system. The truth is that the human-based period of educational reform that began in the '50's is giving way relentlessly, certainly, and inevitably to a second period of educational reform in the United States, and this reform is a technological one.

To use this technology, we must first acquire the proper perspective on the cost of such changes. For example, it is now possible to put a computer console in every elementary school classroom in the United States at a cost of two thousand dollars per console. If we wish to put such a console in every room over a ten-year period, it would cost one billion dollars. That is a lot of money, but through that one billion dollars, we would save five billion, educationally. Furthermore, if we should decide to do this, the cost of the computers in classrooms would drop immediately from two thousand dollars to one thousand just because of the competition. Then, of course, if we decided to put the computer console in the home rather than in the classroom, the cost would be reduced immediately to that of a small television set.

Thus, the use of such equipment is not a dream; it is not even something over which educators really have control. This technological evolution is a social phenomenon that will move relentlessly into the educative process in one way or another. We may resist it for a long time in the schools, only to discover that it is going on elsewhere. For example, we are now graduating our first television generation of students, students who have had television all their lives. These students have been in front of television sets for 15,000 hours by the time they graduate from high school; they have been in school only 12,000 hours during that period of time.

In light of this and similar phenomena, educators must learn to live with these machines. The only way we are going to do this in a rational way is to deliberately create experimental schools into which we introduce all the technology we can think of and study the process of human beings and machines living together.

At the same time though, we must be cognizant of the negative implications of this technological evolution. A personal example will serve to illustrate the human results of this evolution. When I was in Japan, I was intrigued by the fact that although the hotels have automatic elevators, there was always one elevator operated by a young Japanese girl, and I found myself subconsciously waiting for that elevator. I soon realized what I was doing. Going up in an elevator by yourself is a lonely experience.

Thus, we must constantly strive to ease the increasing sense of alienation and loss of identity. There are many humanizing things we could be doing to prevent the development of these feelings. One of them, of course, would be to have little children come to school on their birthday so that the first experience of school would not be with 25 others in a classroom — all brawling, all frightened. Why don't we instead admit children singly on their birthdays and welcome them with a party so that the youngster becomes on the receiving end and then on the giving end? We would thus make clear at the outset the fact that this is an individual and we are going to have to provide a differentiated program for him at a differentiated rate of speed.

Intervening in Human Evolution

The most frightening of all problems results from the development of means of intervening in human evolution. We are now able most effectively to interfere with human evolution through drugs, pot, and such psychedelics as LSD, and we do not really know the potentiality of such outside factors, even though fundamental research on their effects on human behavior is underway. Research is also underway to determine the effects on human evolution of other induced factors. For example, research is being undertaken in regard to chemical transplantation; chemicals from the brains of trained rats are transplanted into the brains of untrained rats to find out how certain training is transferred, enabling the untrained rats to behave in some respects like the trained rats. There is work going on that contrasts the responses and reactions of slow-learning animals to those of rapid-learning animals. The possibilities of the use of electrodes on the brain are being explored.

These techniques are now being used in relation to human deviation. We might not quarrel too much with the use of drugs, chemicals, electrodes, and so on, with a youngster who is severely neurally handicapped or severely emotionally handicapped, but who is emotionally handicapped? Are we the norm in this room? Is there another possible norm for human processes that might emerge in the future? When we talk about deviates and subsequent intervention, we must remember that we all deviate to some degree.

THE CHANGING SCHOOLS

In this discussion of goals, problems, and issues, there is one implicit message. Schools not only must change, they will change. Some of the above indications suggest that they are changing in such a way that there will be no need, for example, for an entrance age any more because a youngster can learn with a computer console put in the home as early as he is able to respond in any way whatsoever. Entrance age is just a convention. There will also be no need for 6-3-3 plans and no need for a 9:00 AM-to-3:00 PM school day. The school day is a convention for the human beings who have to run it, since some kind of a reasonable schedule has to be provided for the human teachers. If human teachers do not have to be scheduled for all learning, there can be around-the-clock learning with the computer console.

A balance of subjects at each level of education is also nothing more than a response, determined again by the availability of human teachers — so many in English, so many in social studies, so many in math, so many in science. We no longer need to observe that convention. It is perfectly possible now for some youngsters to be completely absorbed in a subject six weeks or three months. Many youngsters learn best that way, and there is no reason whatsoever why they shouldn't. Grades, too, are a meaningless convention that can be eliminated.

Too often the role of teachers is also merely a static convention. Teacher roles must change concurrently with the use of machines. Human beings can do certain tasks; machines can do other kinds of tasks. The problem is to find out who can do what. Saying that the computer will do our routine duties and human beings will be left to do the truly human tasks is meaningless. My observation of the computer in education so far is that many teachers are reduced to less human activities by becoming managers of computer data. What the truly human duties are is never specified because we do not know what they are.

The school building also must be profoundly changed. Schools presently being designed without computer cables are obsolete before they are built. It is even possible that every school building is out of date before it is built and that we should not be building them at all.

Already General Learning Corporation is working with the University of California to design a community called Irvine, California, which will incorporate a total planning system and by the end of this century support a population equal to that of Los Angeles. The educational component of the planning system will be geared to serve the entire population from infancy through old age.

Indeed, all education in the future will commence in the home. It will also commence in a generating agency where teachers will spend weeks, perhaps, preparing a half-hour lesson that will be used by millions of youngsters. This is a profoundly different concept that may not require the monstrosity we call a school building, which is recognizable around the world as a prison.

Thus, it is the business of schools to change, and they will change. The major concern is not to become ensnared in dialogue over trivial issues. Let us not involve our communities merely in the little things. Let us instead raise the dialogue to these four questions:

1. To what extent is the child acquiring a meaningful grasp of his culture and a capacity to deal with it?
2. To what extent is each unique individual being esteemed and developed?
3. To what extent is the individual developing a true sense of personal worth?
4. To what extent is the youngster developing some sense of mankind's values?

And there is one question above all others that I want to raise, a question that must be considered as primary in all future educational dialogues. It is not, "What knowledge is of most worth?" It is, "What kinds of human beings do we want to produce?" Put on one pair of glasses, and the future is pretty frightening. Put on another, and it is an exciting challenge to all of us.

Innovation and Teacher Roles

J. Lloyd Trump

INNOVATIONS SUCH AS the utilization of team teaching, independent study, large-group instruction, small-group discussion, flexible scheduling, teacher assistants, new or revised curriculum content, and new technical aids in teaching and learning are widespread. We now know how to overcome the barriers of the educational setting. Actually, it is relatively simple to organize schools differently than they have been. Curriculum content can be arranged logically in a nongraded, continuous progress sequence. Teachers can work in a variety of types of teams to break the isolation of self-contained classrooms. Rigid time divisions can be replaced easily by flexible schedules — some schools now even make up their timetables daily or weekly. Students can easily be regrouped into classes of 100 or more for some activities and into classes of 15 or fewer for other activities; they also can be scheduled for extended periods of time into resource centers for independent study. Teachers can use clerks, instruction assistants, general aides, and technical devices effectively.

All of these modifications are occurring in schools. Although it takes knowledge and courage to make these changes, the big problem lies elsewhere. The challenge is for teachers to learn new instructional roles to go with these changes. Unless teachers learn and adopt new roles, their teaching, and resultant pupil learning, will be little better or different from the past. It is no wonder that the evaluation of most of these innovations fails to reveal significant differences in pupil learning. In most cases, teaching methods and schools have not changed basically; superficial trappings have merely been altered.

To illustrate the changed teaching roles, methods, and behavior required by educational innovations, three crucially important educational goals should be examined at length: individualizing pupil learning, professionalizing teaching, and refining curriculum content. These terms are almost educational clichés. They have been urged and described for many years. Unfortunately too much hazy thinking and timid effort, as well as the existing school settings and practices, have blocked progress toward reaching these goals.

INDIVIDUALIZING PUPIL LEARNING

If the school is to effectively individualize pupil learning, five changes or innovations are essential. The first of these changes is the expansion and alteration of the school's provisions for independent study.

Independent Study

Independent study can be defined very simply: It is what pupils do when their teachers stop talking. Teachers must remind themselves constantly that their job is not to cover a subject but to assist their students to do so. The purpose of teacher talk — done either personally or by means of a film, TV program, or otherwise — is to motivate pupils to learn what they need to learn, to challenge the creativity and the special interests of pupils to go beyond the required minimums, to provide information not readily available elsewhere, and to make assignments so that each pupil may engage successfully in independent study.

Teachers need to understand that independent study has two dimensions: insuring that the pupil covers what the school requires of anyone who is educable and stimulating creativity and depth in studying.

Recognition of individual differences among pupils requires the school to give them much more time outside of regular class groups to engage in independent study. The purpose of this activity is to develop personal responsibility in pupils as they experience learning with maximum self-direction. Although pupils engaged in independent study may work individually or in groups of two, three, ten, or more, the aim is still individual progress.

Teachers should provide the time and a variety of places for productive independent study. This necessitates a great reduction of time spent in organized groups. Instead of teachers meeting with 25 to 35 pupils for each subject each day, such meetings need not occur more than three times a week at most. Students would then spend the rest of the time in independent study, each working at his own level with materials that especially stimulate him. Thus, the amount of independent study determines the degree of the school's attention to individual differences.

Provisions for Continuous Progress

In conventional classrooms, bright pupils often are bored because they have to wait for others to catch up, and less-talented pupils are frustrated because the pace is too fast for them. This arrangement contrasts sharply to individualized learning situations in which each pupil can successfully complete each stage in the learning process and then go on to the next without delay.

Such a nongraded program not only requires administrative changes in a school but also a different arrangement of curricular content and variations in the nature of the teacher's assignments. Guide sheets and oral instructions tell pupils with varied talents and interests what each of them need and can do. The accompanying work sheets provide alternative ways to do an assignment. Teachers then analyze pupil progress to evaluate the effectiveness of their assignments and the provisions for independent study.

Discussion Skills and Interpersonal Relations

Different teacher roles and class organization are also needed to teach how to express ideas in an effective oral manner, to listen to the ideas of others in order to react positively to them, to argue and to identify areas of agreement and disagreement, and to respect other pupils and gain their respect in the process. Today's conventional classrooms cannot provide the optimum setting or the right teacher roles needed for these goals. The maximum number in discussion groups must not exceed 12 to 15 if each pupil is to have an opportunity to express himself in the reasonable length of time that the group meets.

The teacher role thus changes from lecturer, quizzer, teacher–pupil planner, and organizer of other activities to that of observer, critic of the effectiveness of the discussion, and helper. This change in the teacher role is effected by teaching discussion techniques, evaluating the results, and reconstituting the groups from time to time, not only to improve interpersonal relations among pupils but to provide each pupil with the optimum opportunity to learn how to express ideas and listen to others. Such goals simply cannot be achieved effectively in conventional classes where the focus cannot be placed adequately on the individual because the group is too large and the teacher is too much in charge.

Individualized Evaluation

Another hindrance to the individualization of pupil learning is created by present evaluation practices. The following are three present evaluation practices teachers should stop immediately.

The first, and most crucial, is the constant comparison of the individual with other pupils in whatever group he happens to be. Instead, the evaluation to be emphasized should be the individual pupil's progress or lack of it. The comparisons needed are between what the individual is doing or knows today as related to accomplishments of a month ago, six months ago, or longer. Comparing a pupil with others in his group may give the relatively successful a false sense of security; it is almost certain to give the failing pupils a continuing sense of frustration and defeat.

A second practice to abandon is the oral quizzing of pupils in groups. This practice embarrasses some individuals and, conversely, enhances the already felt superiority of others. Moreover, teachers now spend one-fourth or more of class time on this activity, time that would be better spent by pupils in independent study and by teachers in professional activities. Better ways than oral quizzing are available to determine rate of learning. Teachers may observe progress as pupils work through programed materials or as two or three pupils work and evaluate together, and they may give occasional written tests or engage in personal conversations with pupils to appraise progress.

Giving pupils multipurpose, single letter grades is the third practice that should be eliminated. What a pupil knows should not be combined with what he can do. His punctuality and attendance record should not be combined with appraisal of his behavior, style of dress, and creativity in special projects. The combined grade violates the recognition of individual differences and determines such matters as rank in class, admission to college, success in job applications, and participation in school activities. Instead the school needs to evaluate and report each aspect of a student's knowledge and behavior separately.

To individualize evaluation, the teacher's roles must change. In every subject teachers need to state their most important purposes in terms that can be quantified, measured, and reported, with each purpose described separately from the others. For example, what does a person who appreciates music do that is different from one who does not? What standards in physical fitness, recreation, and health does the school measure and report for each pupil? How many words per minute can a pupil type with an average of how many errors? The essential question is, what progress is each individual making in all of these areas? Since the teacher lacks time to evaluate everything, he must decide what the highest priorities for the grading period are. He must also decide whether a given purpose should be evaluated by one teacher or by a team of teachers, a team evaluation being preferable in many instances. These evaluation procedures will then influence teaching roles and individual pupil learning.

Relationships with Teachers

Individualizing learning also requires each pupil to have an opportunity to relate to a teacher who is good for him. Today's schools deny pupils that privilege when they require them to be with one teacher in junior or senior high schools all year to complete a subject, or all day for a year in the case of elementary schools. To require a pupil to spend that much time with one teacher whom he may not like or who may not like him interferes with the goal of individualizing learnings. No condemnation of teacher talents is implied; a teacher who is bad for one pupil may be good for another.

Changing the current arrangement necessitates abolishing the self-contained classroom. Instead pupils should be in contact with several teachers, both in group situations and during their independent study. Teachers, too, need to be free from full-time classroom assignments so a pupil, at a given time, can find and talk to the teacher he needs. The goal of individualizing learning can thus be achieved by a variety of methods.

PROFESSIONALIZING TEACHING

Another crucial educational goal that should be considered in depth is that of professionalizing teaching. Teaching organizations are striving to do so and are more vigorously seeking certain long-standing goals. Unfortunately their emphasis is sometimes misplaced. For example, higher salaries and smaller classes are not the two most crucial matters in improving teaching and learning. Higher salaries do help teachers to live better, and they also bring a sense of community and national appreciation. However, higher salaries do not automatically improve teaching and learning.

The same can be said for smaller classes. Reducing the class size or the teacher-pupil ratio in conventional schools from 35 to 32 to 28.5 to 24.4 will not automatically improve pupils' learning or their success in college. This has been shown by many investigations. Reducing pupil numbers does make life somewhat easier for teachers because they then do not have so many papers to grade or so many persons to contend with, but it does not materially change the quality of pupil learning. Conversely, there are at least four changes in teacher roles and school organization that can add both to the professionalization of teaching and to the improvement of pupils' work.

Attention to Individual Differences

One of these changes concerns the individual differences of teachers. Everyone knows that individual differences among teachers exist, but today's schools largely ignore this fact. There are uniform salary schedules, uniform teaching loads, uniform criteria used to measure teacher success, and so on. All of those standardized administrative relationships deny individual differences among teachers.

Each teacher needs a school situation where he may best exercise his individual talents and interests. No longer should teachers be expected to do everything that is needed for a given group of pupils. Team teaching should be utilized, with differentiated functions among teachers, just as the school emphasizes individual differences among pupils. However, this suggestion does not imply a hierarchy of teachers. For example, I have never used the term master teacher because it implies that a teacher is superior in everything and, therefore, should be in charge. Such a concept still denies individual differences because no one teacher is superior in everything.

Auxiliary Personnel

Another fundamental ingredient in professionalizing teaching consists of identifying what professional teachers must do and what may be done by a variety of assistants. Initially different self-concepts and behavior are required to make such assistance effective. Many teachers today appear to have an I-must-do-it-myself complex. They say, in effect: "I must cover the subject. I can do it better than anyone else. I will not be replaced by a machine." All these concepts are wrong to a degree.

Three kinds of assistants are required. Clerks are needed to keep records, check attendance, duplicate materials, grade some objective tests, and the like. Instruction assistants can supervise pupils engaged in independent study in a variety of places and otherwise help teachers in a variety of ways. Such instruction assistants would be persons with some preparation in the subject area and age group that the teacher works with but not necessarily enough training for complete certification. General aides can supervise playgrounds, lunchrooms, and corridors, help small children with clothing, and perform other services that do not require clerical training or the preparation attained by instruction assistants. These auxiliary personnel can perform tasks that now occupy more than one-third of the teacher's time.

Of course, the teacher's relationships with pupils would be changed when auxiliary personnel are employed. Teachers would work with pupils more on the basis of referrals and appointments made by the assistants or by pupils themselves. Rather than performing the tasks themselves, they would analyze reports from the assistants. They would help their pupils understand the purposes of the assistants and how to work with them. Instead of knowing a little about a lot of pupils, the teacher would then know a lot more about a smaller number whom he would serve as teacher–counselor, and he would not have to collect all the data himself.

There can be no real teaching profession until teachers, their students, and the community understand the relationships described in the preceding paragraphs. Certainly, the workers in other professional groups, such as medicine and engineering, have long since abandoned the roles comparable to those that teachers follow in today's schools.

Technical Devices

It is true, too, that today's teachers represent the only so-called professional group that has not escaped from the handwork era. The tools of the typical teacher still include only his physical voice and gestures, a chalkboard, and printed materials. None of us would respect or consult a doctor, engineer, or architect who did not utilize up-to-date technical tools to aid him in his activities.

Teachers need to analyze carefully what they must do themselves and what pupils can learn for themselves through the use of a variety of technical aids to learning. Teachers can enhance their own voices with amplification systems and use visual devices to illuminate their presentations. When a teacher talks, the size of the pupil group is irrelevant so long as each one can see and hear well. To motivate their students, teachers must be reasonably up-to-date in the use of materials that enliven the television programs and motion pictures that pupils are accustomed to seeing outside of school.

There is no shortage of technical devices. Many of them have been around for a half century and more, but they still have not found their way into most instructional programs in the same manner that textbooks are used. Computer-assisted instruction, for example, is already a reality in experimental classrooms, but most teachers are without it, and they possess other technical aids only to a limited degree.

Teachers not only need to accept and learn how to use technical devices, but they also must become militant in stimulating school administrators and boards of education to spend money differently so they can afford to provide the technical devices teachers require. Much money now wasted on poorly conceived school buildings could be saved to purchase technical tools for teaching and pupil learning. The school building itself does little more than provide a comfortable and healthful environment; it is the technical devices that produce better teaching and learning.

Time and Places to Work

Another obstacle in professionalizing teaching arises from the fact that teachers are scheduled with pupil groups most of the school day; they should not be scheduled with pupil groups more than half the school day. Teachers need time to prepare better, to keep up to date, to confer with their professional colleagues and with individual pupils, and to improve the evaluation of their own efforts and the progress of their pupils. Teachers also need their own offices with at least quasi-privacy, rooms for small group meetings and conferences, and places where instructional materials can be prepared with competent persons available to help them.

Today's teachers, too often their supervisors, and even the community seem to believe that a teacher earns his pay only when he is in front of 25 to 35 pupils, book in hand. That concept of the teacher's role must change. Most teachers could function once or twice a week as a presenter, in charge of a relatively large group of pupils. For another 12 to 15 periods a week, the teacher should serve as a consultant or observer of pupils meeting in groups of 15 or fewer, these sessions varying in length, averaging 40 minutes. The rest of the time the teacher should be engaged in a variety of other professional activities, especially those related to independent study and evaluation. In these ways the goal of professionalizing teaching can be attained.

REFINING CURRICULUM CONTENT

The third, and final, major educational goal is the refinement of curriculum content. School innovations and changed teacher roles in curriculum planning and development should include identifying the differences between fundamental or basic materials and those that are in the realm of creativity and special interests. Today's content often confuses those two areas to the extent that pupils find much content required that they neither want nor need. As a result, they often lose interest and sometimes rebel or become underachievers. Even worse, they lack the time and energy to follow their special interests and to develop their unique talents. We need to separate the important kernels from the chaff and get rid of the latter as a required diet for all learners.

Required Learnings

So far as basic education is concerned, teachers and curriculum experts need to identify the facts, concepts, skills, and appreciations that are essential in our society for anyone who is educable. Beyond that minimum, the schools also need to identify the content that is desirable for most people and that which is enriching for the specially talented. It is possible that national groups will identify this curriculum content for all persons in the United States. Then other groups can augment that content by adding materials needed by persons in a given state. Local teachers will complete the content by adding materials regarded as essential for the particular community and region.

The foregoing fundamental content needs to be arranged logically and sequentially so that the continuous progress of pupils is facilitated. This required work should be held to a minimum so that there is time for additional study in areas where individuals have special talents and interests.

Creativity and Depth

The teacher role in motivating, providing extra information, and making assignments is to suggest what pupils may do to go beyond the fundamental or required content in creative ways or in greater depth. Such a program eliminates the outmoded "required-and-elective" system, which often limits the breadth of experience for pupils in the upper years, keeping them away, for example, from fine and practical arts or specialized work in mathematics or literature. The average pupil might complete the essential required content by the time he is 16 years of age, so that his basic education beyond that occupies only 10 to 20 per cent of his school time. He, of course, would always need some time to keep up to date, refresh his memory, or correct wrong information learned earlier. Beyond that requirement, he would devote the rest of his time to creativity and depth studies for the world of work or advanced studies leading to the university.

So far as content is concerned, the teacher's role is to use what has been developed nationally and regionally. He should not waste time on decision-making in this regard but should accept or criticize what the experts have done. His major efforts should concern the local content that is added to the basic education and the development of meaningful and productive creative and depth educational programs for his pupils.

SOME ADDITIONAL CONSIDERATIONS

Refining curriculum content, professionalizing teaching, and individualizing pupil learning are the three crucially important educational goals today. In viewing educational innovations, however, there are also other necessary considerations. One is that of educational facilities.

Educational Facilities

Today's schools largely relegate decisions about educational facilities, buildings, grounds, supplies, equipment, and money to supervisors and administrators. Teachers only give advice when requested to do so.

Innovations require changes in the way that money is spent and facilities are utilized. Boards of education and school administrators need to change their perspectives about facilities in order to encourage innovations and to support them adequately, and teachers need to help in this process.

A school district so disposed can easily save enough money while constructing a new building or remodeling an old one to purchase needed technical aids to teaching and learning in quantities far beyond those which are provided today. Teachers can then have the services of assistants, a schedule that provides time for professional activities, classes of 15 or fewer pupils, and the like, without adding to the district's tax burden.

Educational Innovation

In viewing educational innovations, one might also ask, "What is an educational innovation and why?" A friend recently said that where he came from, the term could be used to describe panic bars placed on the school's exit doors. Yet in other places, dial-access systems are considered less innovative than computerized carrels. The simple dictionary definition, "something new or different," is scarcely adequate for decision-making in education. A conceptual basis is required to categorize and evaluate educational innovations.

Too many schools adopt innovations mainly because others are doing so. Thus, the only questions asked in some schools are, "What is *in* this year, and how can we sell it to teachers, students, and the community?"

But there are fundamental guidelines for considering educational innovations. Moreover, the effectiveness of any educational innovation in comparison with the practice it replaced must be judged on the basis of such fundamental guidelines as the following:

1. The educational innovation furthers these three fundamental goals — individualizing learning, professionalizing teaching, and refining content.

2. The innovation is viewed in relation to other aspects of teaching and learning.

3. Evaluation of the innovation requires different techniques for analyzing what happens to pupils, teachers, and content.

4. The innovation constitutes making fundamental changes rather than following a fad.

5. The innovation requires that teachers and pupils have different roles, methods, and behavior.

Finally, two generalizations about educational innovations may be derived from this presentation. Hopefully, these should spur principals, teachers, and those that support them to intensive study and action. First, there is little inherent magic in the educational innovations that most of us urge. That is the reason why in so many cases the evaluations show no significant differences in pupil learning, even though the teachers and pupils enjoy the changes that television, independent study, flexible schedules, and the like bring. Second, basic improvements in teaching, learning, and content cannot be made effectively in the framework of the one-teacher, thirty-pupil self-contained classrooms or with the six or seven period day. However, schools will not be made better merely by reducing the teacher-pupil ratio, diminishing the number of pupils per day for English teachers, or adding calculus, four years of a foreign language, or any other extra courses to the overcrowded curriculum of the conventional secondary school. These superficial arrangements will not improve teaching, learning, and content to any marked degree.

Schools in the United States and in other countries can be improved mightily. We possess in the latter third of the 20th century the know-how to individualize learning, professionalize teaching, and refine content. The questions that must be asked are, "Do we have the patience, the willingness, and the drive to change teacher roles, methods, and behavior? Will principals develop a staff organization to free themselves from the trivia of management details so they can work with teachers to improve instruction? Will university researchers come out of their cloisters to work with schools to improve teaching and learning?" If the answer to these questions is affirmative and the action required is effected, then we can and will attain our crucial educational goals to the betterment of all.

Teacher Training and Selection

Donald N. Bigelow

SCHOOLS ARE FOR CHILDREN. This simple statement is the one fundamental fact on which there is universal agreement in any consideration of the multifaceted problems facing American education today. In the classroom a child develops and grows as the result of a series of interactions between teacher and pupil. It would appear to be a logical corollary that if a student fails to achieve to his full potential, this failure should be attributed to the errors and shortcomings of the school. More bluntly, it is the teacher and not the child who should be blamed for the failure.

Our purpose is not to celebrate innovations scattered hither and thither but to treat a fundamental problem in American education and of American society — what changes will make for better schools? My particular concern is with those transactions that take place between teacher and student, viewed within a framework in which the point of reference is the teacher and not the child. This is a framework in which the consumer is not blamed for the failure of the product.

In regard to these transactions, there are three components of the educational universe involved: elementary and secondary schools, colleges and universities, and the state. Until we talk about change that actively involves all three, all other change is likely to be isolated and largely ineffective.

We cannot allow ourselves to talk about change in a vacuum, whether the vacuum be a school, a state education agency, or an institution of higher education. If we are going to be logicians, tacticians, and strategists, we must begin looking at the full scope of the educational universe.

INTERACTION BETWEEN TEACHERS AND STUDENTS

Until we look forcefully and honestly at the interaction that takes place between the student and the teacher, in conjunction with the state as well as higher education, there will be no real change possible in the school system. Surely if the school must communicate with the community that surrounds it, then it must also relate to the other two components of the educational enterprise.

In this necessary reconstruction of American education, I have my own notions about the direction in which we should move. We should begin by dispensing with the special categories of education such as pre-school, early childhood, kindergarten, and elementary. These categories are all one and the same. Thus, elementary education should begin with age three and continue through age eight, in five grades.

The nine-year-old would then enter the sixth grade and seven years later would finish the twelfth grade at the age of 16, having completed 12 grades in 14 calendar years but still emerging from secondary education two years earlier than usual.

Next, there would be three years of college, this being accomplished by eliminating the last year at the four-year institutions and adding a third year to every community and junior college. To keep pace with the demands of our technological society and the needs of the students of tomorrow, the liberal arts would include the industrial arts or vocational education and the business of teaching *and* learning. Thus, the university would be free to play its major role — the acquisition of knowledge and the dedication to scholarship that is the basis of professionalism.

To initiate these changes, all people who teach special education would immediately leave the field and begin teaching at the elementary level, since these people have the kind of training needed to teach the young child. Next, all men would leave the secondary schools for the elementary schools. Finally, most of the categories that now stigmatize so many children, separating them from their fellows and leaving them to the attention of the growing ranks of specialists, would be discarded.

But all these steps merely constitute, after all, another change, and it's no better than any of the changes already tried because the essential ingredient is missing. Nothing has been done about the problem of the interaction that takes place between the teacher and the student. Yet this is really the nub of the problem.

In considering this interaction, it is necessary first to generalize about teachers and teaching. In the first place, it is not true that teachers are born and not made. Quite the contrary. But it is true that teaching is an art, an art that is, in many instances, born. Some acquire it by birth, or by environmental influences, or by a combination of both. The problem is that there are not enough such teachers to meet our needs, so we are faced with the problem of training good teachers, and that is what we are not doing.

WHY GOOD TEACHERS ARE NOT BEING TRAINED

We are not doing it for a variety of reasons. We are not doing it largely because we are not really concerned with the teacher, not concerned enough to attract men of dedication and conviction to teaching. We employ a whole host of remedial people to take care of what the teacher doesn't do and to solve problems that the administration doesn't seem able to handle. We utilize many special educationalists, counselors, and remedial reading specialists, but each of them is like the little boy with his finger in the dyke. For that matter, all of us are in that posture, comforting ourselves by solving the smallest problem in front of us, practicing the most primitive methods of flood control possible. To put it another way, we have allowed our vision to be obscured by at least four massive red herrings of American education.

The first red herring is the present preoccupation with innovation. There is nothing wrong with innovating. Clearly, everything in our system calls for it, and our schools are made better by virtue of it. But it is in this context a red herring, since it usually takes us farther away from the point of talking about the transaction between teachers and learners. For example, team teaching is an innovation of great possible merit, and changing the school physically to accommodate this innovation is also worthwhile. But it really doesn't matter whether we knock the walls out of the room to create new architectural forms unless we people them with good teachers. Certainly it is a problem to acquire good teachers, but the fact is that the schools do not insist upon them, and this is the basic weakness in the system.

Curriculum development is another red herring. Curriculum development is a fine goal, but it takes us away from our consideration of the major matter, and sometimes it only adds to the miseries of the teacher. I've never seen a good teacher who didn't tear up a curriculum and then reconstruct his own. There's much too much wall-to-wall curriculum development built on the assumption that a teacher wouldn't know what to do without it. Therefore, when you look in that direction, your eyes are straying from the true point of focus.

The third red herring is educational technology. There is nothing wrong with using these educational devices if they are convenient and practical. There is nothing the matter with a good hot light on you if you don't mind perspiring. There is nothing the matter with an overhead projector if you can find the plug when you want it. But educational technology is merely a supplement to the skills of a good teacher; it cannot be regarded as a substitute for that teacher.

The last, and most important, red herring is scholarship, since we have allowed ourselves to become victims of it. It seems strange that two thousand years of scholarship, without which our civilization certainly would have perished, has, paradoxically, become a force that has stultified teaching.

What has happened under the aegis of scholarship? Our great universities and those that want to be great want to be so on one basis — obtain that scholar. What is really the business of the scholar? To acquire knowledge. Who is against it? No one, but we must not be victimized by it. We must understand that today the average college teacher in the average university probably is not the least bit concerned with the problem of teaching and, unfortunately, probably doesn't teach very well. This whole business of apprenticeship, in which we learn by watching the master, is a palpable fraud. To learn the devices of scholarship without participating in the substance of it is not the business of the school.

These remarks are not a condemnation of the university any more than they are a condemnation of innovation, curriculum development, or educational technology. Innovation certainly can be productive; curriculum reform may be needed; and educational media and computerized instruction will ultimately affect every classroom in the land. But we must set our values straight. Within our framework of reference, the preparation of teachers of excellence in the university, devoted as it is to scholarship, is not succeeding. In the words of Dr. William Arrowsmith, Professor of Classics at the University of Texas, "At present the universities are as uncongenial to teaching as the Mojave Desert to a clutch of Druid priests."

"The present state of affairs," Dr. Arrowsmith wrote, is "a vast educational enterprise built entirely upon a case of learned men whose learning has no relevance to the young and even seems to alienate the young from both education and culture. It is a vision of madness accomplished."

Out of this madness then, how do you obtain the teachers you need? There must be a way to find people and hire people who know about children and who can teach them. There is. But the schools may have to serve as the catalyst for the development of such people. First, we must know what we should expect the teachers to learn who will be coming to our schools. Then we must look to the source from which the teacher comes, the college and university. That is the reason why we must consider the triad of the school, the state, and the university. If the university is not delivering what is needed, the fault lies with the school and the state, for elementary and secondary education is the greatest consumer of the university's *en bloc* output. Mass purchasing power should be able to buy what it wants, prescribe standards of quality, and decline to accept that which fails to meet specifications. Translated into the marketplace of education, that means standards of what teachers should be. If necessary, we must treat the university like Macy's. We must go to Macy's and buy what we need. But we must know exactly what we need before we go to buy it. If we are strong enough, it will be provided.

In the over-the-counter bargaining that will inevitably be involved, educators should not look to the federal government or even to the professional organizations for any real support. In these matters the federal government may stimulate, but it does not have and should not have the machinery to implement such ideas locally. The professional associations may profess dedication to the cause of effective change, but one is never certain whether their concern is for teaching or scholarship.

It is the school system that has the need, and that is where the action must begin. The great change will come when the community looks not to the federal government but to the state and to the local colleges and universities and says to them, "I demand a teacher."

The Subordination of Teaching to Learning

Caleb Gattegno

AN APPROACH TO EDUCATION that completely recasts the classroom techniques in all subjects is certainly an all-encompass-
ing innovation. I am promulgating just such an approach, one
I call "the subordination of teaching to learning." Fundamentally this approach necessitates the realization by the educator
that the student brings certain skills and understandings with
him to school and that he learns by functioning, just as one
learns how to drive. The resulting techniques of education
and the approach itself demand some justification. To understand and believe in such an approach, we first must rid ourselves of the following two basic misconceptions about learning that underlie the present system of education: one learns
by imitation, and one retains learning through memory.

INADEQUACY OF THE LEARNING-BY-IMITATION THEORY

Many years ago I noted that verbal communication is at
best a kind of incantation and at worst a vehicle for sheer confusion. Words are only the medium of communication and
not the message. As Talleyrand said, "Language has been
given man in order to disguise his thoughts." Assuming this to

be valid, a very special intellectual contortion is required to extract from spoken or written words the true meaning that one wishes to convey through their use.

All of us are masters in the use of speech, in spite of all its shortcomings. And since this mastery is achieved very early in life, we rarely examine the reality of speech and the many fascinating features we have incorporated into it over the centuries as mankind and over the years as individuals. For our purpose here, it will suffice to notice two facts about speech. One is that a vaguely felt intention is sufficient to organize all our mental functionings, including some somatic ones such as the movements of our lips and tongue, and to produce a flow of words that is recognized after the event as being on the whole adequate insofar as the grammar and the syntax of the language used and possessing the pronunciation and intonations needed to convey implicitly the meanings intended. The other truth about speech is that it has not been taught to us and that it was acquired at a very tender age.

Thus, in the field of speech, we all act in an extremely complex manner (of which detailed knowledge is not available). We act creatively, originally, and purposefully, using a very abstract medium, since words are symbols that have little to do with what they represent. Words are classes and represent indefinite numbers of objects, possibilities, and so forth; furthermore, words are used in highly sophisticated spatial and temporal situations and are often used ambiguously or interchangeably.

For example, it is commonly said that children learn to talk by imitation — they say what they hear. The following simple test will disprove this belief. Were I to ask one of two persons, "Could you please tell the other person what you would call the item on my face to which I am pointing?" he would answer, "Your nose." Turning to the other person, I would say, "Please touch your nose." If the person touches his nose, then obviously he does not use imitation, since the label "your nose" was used for *this* item on *my* face. Had he touched my nose, as would be required for the learning-by-imitation theory to be valid, how could he explain the fact that, as a child, he had learned to change possessive adjectives as required by speech?

Indeed, to use speech requires the use of a dynamic set of schemas that are highly organized by criteria. These criteria must be possessed by anyone who speaks fluently, since changes occur automatically as soon as one's head turns, or a new intention arises, or the same action is seen against the flow of time. This last awareness is necessary for the change of moods and tenses that take place all the time when we talk to each other.

Whoever has tried to learn a skill merely by watching someone who uses it masterfully knows how difficult it is to benefit from watching. In the past, apprenticeship in a trade guild took many years, probably because students were asked to learn by imitating successes of the master. Man learns far more easily from his errors than from his successes. Mistakes arouse his awareness and permit him to move from where he is to where he should be.

DISCRIMINATING USE OF MENTAL POWERS FROM BIRTH

Nearly everyone has mastered the spoken speech of his environment by the age of four or five to a degree of excellence that is definitely amazing. The main point to be derived from this commonplace experience is that *we all have extraordinary mental powers that we know how to use effectively, discriminately, and inventively almost from birth.* This lesson we must all learn. All of us, as babies, were surrounded by people who used speech as an integrated tool, automatically, and to their satisfaction; we did not notice the shortcomings that existed in this speech when compared with the most cultured one used in the community. We made sense on our own of what people meant when talking, and we taught ourselves this subtle and complicated skill without outside help.

Every one of us should be proud of this achievement, and we should be very proud of this display of power in every child. But this immediately raises a whole set of difficult challenges: Can I learn from this very common event something about how man functions when acquiring skills of all kinds? Can I do justice to everyone's powers in the work of people I have to direct as an educator? Can I recast my inherited culture — which stems from assumptions about man other than the ones I must consider today — so that I am able to meet the future as it is?

Two other challenging questions also arise: (1) Is it possible to view history in a new light since what we believed only some people capable of doing, can now be considered within the reach of everyone? and (2) What kind of education can be proposed today and in the immediate future that will enable us to remain true to reality?

ROLES OF MEMORY AND FUNCTIONING

The Schools for the Future, founded in 1965, have studied these challenges, and the result is a new approach to education.

In light of that study and the challenges it met, we must also revise our ideas on the role of memory in learning. Does it not seem extraordinary that although all of us learn through experience not to trust our memories, we still believe that our school learning, our acquisition of knowledge, should be based on memory? No one here remembers his mother tongue. It is too useful an instrument to base its dynamic retention on memory. The process that is used, in fact, can be termed functioning.

This is true for any of the other skills. Your driving or your reading are not memorized; they are at your disposal, and they can be performed to fit any particular circumstances. If to remember means to know something in all the transformations that are compatible with it, then the word memory can be used. But the track left on a record or a tape is more descriptive of what ordinarily is called memory, because we seem to require from it faithfulness, fidelity, and a close reproduction of the original statement.

Since the power of man's memory is to forget, to cast off the irrelevant, we must not be surprised that most of us have kept very little of what we entrusted to our memory at school and elsewhere. Ask yourselves seriously how relevant to your functionings were so many of the lessons you learned by heart at school.

ACQUIRING SKILLS AND UNDERSTANDING

The subjects we meet in school can be classified as either skills or understandings. Both are linked in a number of ways, but they are sufficiently different to be considered separately. The primary difference is that learning skills demands concentration, while achievement of understanding requires cultivating sensitivity to others, the world, mathematics, beauty, and so on.

Skills such as writing involve us much more than subjects such as history. In the first, we must reach a level where we can perform all of it, while in the second, we must hold the retelling of events — of which we can know only very little — at a place in our mind where nothing may happen to alter it. We must be able to command the first but must keep the other unchanged.

Skills at school include various uses of oneself as: a listener, looker, talker, walker, climber; as a writer, speller, composer, transcriber of feelings; as a reckoner, image-maker, and imaginer; and many more. These skills may have already been developed to some extent before children come to school, and we need to take this into account. We also need to see to what extent the child's already acquired skills and understandings can be used, thus enabling the learner to reach a high level of responsible functioning much faster than when his existing knowledge is neglected.

SUBORDINATING TEACHING TO LEARNING

This approach to education is subordinating teaching to learning. Let us take an example to contrast the traditional way of teaching to the one I am proposing. If some five-year-olds can say that 5 plus 5 is another name for 10 — the denary system — we would usually expect them to know that 5 apples plus 5 apples make 10 apples, but we would not think of asking them what 5 hundred (or thousand, or million, or billion) plus 5 hundred (or thousand, etc.) make. Anyone who can say 10 apples as the answer to the first question can say 10 hundred, or 10 thousand, and so on because this is a power that he has already shown he possesses. From the point of view of the powers of the mind, we are not here considering 10 billion or 10 million billion as a number but as a pattern of sounds; and through this exercise we have acquired more of the extent covered by the equivalence "5 plus 5 is another name for 10." On the other hand, we have traditionally believed that "7 plus 7 as equivalent to 14" is a fact to be retained independently of "8 plus 8 as equivalent to 16."

To function according to the new approach would require that we retain as little as possible, but that we know and understand how to generate answers one from another, via controlled transformations.

A study of the minimum that needs to be retained can yield some remarkable information. For instance, to know all addition facts with integers in our common denary system, we need to retain the following table:

1	2	3	4	5	6	7	8	9
10	20	30	40	50	60	70	80	90
100	200	300	400	500	600	700	800	900

This requires remembering nine labels for the top line, the four irregular ones and the sound *ty* for the second, and the label *hundred* for the third, plus the irregular *eleven, twelve, thirteen, fifteen,* and *teen;* that is, 20 labels in all to form 999 numerals. If we add the names for two commas in the classical notation, namely *thousand* between 1,000 and 999,999 and *million* between 1,000,000 and 999,999,999, this addition of two labels to the 20 we already have will extend the reading and writing of numerals up to 999,999,999.

In using this method of learning, the mental powers of the students, rather than their ages, shape the syllabus. It is clear that not only can we in this way restore sense to arithmetic, but we can also bring to our students' attention vast areas of experience whenever the same patterns prevail, and we do this without increasing our demands on their time.

It is obvious that once we become preoccupied with considerations of this type, it becomes possible to make pedagogical discoveries that are impossible otherwise. For instance, I can now say that it only takes six years to master what is supposed to require 12 years today in mathematics. Moreover, the vast majority of students can perform at this higher level and enjoy doing so, at no great cost to themselves.

Using this system, I developed appropriate materials for teaching trigonometry. Utilizing color films, I was able to store into nine minutes of screening time the material necessary for everyone to know all the important aspects of the trigonometry course, for which months are usually required and which at present reaches only a small percentage of students.

However spectacular its contribution to mathematics learning seemed, this new approach, when applied to reading, produced the almost incredible result that it takes only a matter of hours — sometimes less than 10 — to master its techniques. These, in turn, quickly lead to fluent reading with comprehension, thus satisfying the demands of the most exacting teachers. Moreover the age at which children can begin to learn to read may be lowered to four.

To facilitate learning English, which is highly nonphonetic, we may need more time, perhaps 20 to 25 hours. With remedial groups, the time taken can vary from one to eight or ten hours, as we prove regularly in our clinic in New York City. These statements can be made because we know that if we let children show us what they can do, we discover that since they have made sense of speech on their own, they can very quickly make sense of its codification in writing.

Spelling, however, is a different matter. Spelling can be conquered very quickly too, but it requires techniques different from those that lead to the mastery of reading. To read is to obtain the meaning contained in a text in the same way one obtains the meaning of speech. To know words as such, which is necessary for correct spelling, goes counter to reading for meaning. To succeed in spelling requires acquiring a certain imagery and its dynamics, the techniques of which have also been developed.

The basic skills of reading, writing, spelling, and mathematics of numbers and operations can easily be presented in a manner that will enable every pupil to contribute to the maximum and to take full responsibility during his apprenticeship. This will lead him to mastery and the application of his acquired know-how to a variety of situations.

Can one go beyond this? The answer is yes. I have developed the approach of subordinating teaching to learning in foreign languages. The skill aspects of science and the social sciences can be treated likewise. It is also possible to use this approach in music, art, and physical education, since, to a great extent, these are skill subjects.

In enabling students to learn foreign languages, "The Silent Way" — with which I have been experimenting in many countries since 1954 — seems to be the first scientific approach to the challenge, and it has made a big difference to students of all ages. Here again, functioning is the key. Learners from the start and always thereafter are asked to rely on memory only when it is required — which is rarely. Instead, criteria are developed in their minds that help them acquire a progressively greater degree of discrimination and independence. In this way, functioning will be attained. Subordinating teaching to learning also produces greater yields in this area of instruction.

EDUCATION AS A SCIENCE

However interesting all this may be, the most important contribution to education that such insights can make is that we can now consider education as a science, as well as the art it certainly is.

A science is neutral, unbiased, fair and honest, useful, and inescapable. In the science of education, we can now take into account the learners. We have, therefore, restored this component of the process to its place and, by so doing, have shown that we have become more effective and more realistic.

It so happens that by being more realistic, we have gone beyond the dreams of the most optimistic idealist in the field. And this is no longer a matter of belief, but a fact. The fact is that every time we know what we are doing and how and why it works, we give everyone his proper chance, and we are able to work together rather than against one another.

Is this not an innovation? And the future holds more in store. For example, I am presently engaged in finding the rightful place, in the process of improving yields in education, of the various ways of knowing that mankind has developed. It will be as useless to ignore imagery — as has been done for centuries when words dominated education — as it will be to believe that man is only eyes. Man is complex, and the future unknown. We can only throw bridges ahead, with one end supported in the present and the other looking for the firm future on which to settle.

The Humanities in Transition

Harry L. Levy

WHEN ADAM WAS LEAVING the garden with Eve, he turned to her and remarked, "You must remember, my dear, that we are living in a period of transition!" For humanity itself, as distinguished from the humanities, has always been in a period of transition — in that state of flux that, as Heraclitus observed long ago, is characteristic of all things.

Transition is, like every other form of movement, a relative matter. It is the change of position of X with respect to Y; it all depends upon one's point of view. Here, I am regarding the humanities as a fairly stable entity, with modern man in transition with respect to them. By the term humanities I mean, of course, the results of literary and artistic creation that have survived the passing centuries and have come down to us as an acknowledged part of our cultural heritage.

This transition, for Western man at least, is a change from a situation in which the humanities were the universally accepted core of education for all those who went beyond the most elementary stages of learning to a situation in which the humanities must compete for the student's attention with complex and varied bodies of thought and knowledge in the fields of natural and social sciences.

When the humanities were central to the secondary and

higher education curriculums in the Western world, they provided a basis for communication and common understanding for educated men throughout the Western lands. They provided a frame of reference that could be used, and was used, with sureness and certainty of understanding by the relatively small number of men in previous centuries who had occasion to communicate on intellectual and abstract subjects.

Rather than engaging in fruitless nostalgia for a bygone substructure of communication, however, I will attempt to discuss two things: (1) the means of conserving and communicating the values of the humanities for the participants of our present-day culture, and (2) the task of preserving and, to the extent possible, of strengthening existing modes of intellectual and abstract communication in a manner that is practicable and suitable for our times.

But what of innovation? There is no innovation involved in the basic idea of conserving and communicating the values of the humanities in the setting of each succeeding generation. That is what the teachers of literature have done since the Greeks began to learn Homer as their basic text. Each generation of teachers of the humanities must itself learn the heritage of the past. This, of necessity, involves a close study of language: either a foreign language — the Romans learned Greek, the Italians learned Greek and Latin — or an earlier stage of one's own language — the Greeks of Plato's time learned the language of Homer, our teachers of English learn the language of Chaucer, Spenser, and Shakespeare.

INNOVATIONS IN LEARNING FOREIGN LANGUAGES

The learning of foreign languages does, however, open before us a wide field for innovation. It was my personal privilege to be involved, some 22 years ago, in the innovative efforts of American linguists in the area of language learning.

As a student in the Military Intelligence Chinese Language School at Yale, I experienced firsthand what was then a startling innovation but has now become fairly commonplace — the substitution of pattern–practice, based upon structural linguistic analysis, for the centuries-old grammar-translation method of teaching and learning languages. Sound-scribers and wire-recorders were the hardware for our lessons; the tape recorder had yet to become common. A set of new textbooks with pattern–practice in the structure of the target language was the software. Both hardware and software seem, in retrospect, primitive, since we have advanced so far in less than a quarter-century. Nevertheless, they worked surprisingly well. Some of us, in four months of intensive work, were able to learn more Chinese than the French we had learned in eight years of conventional courses.

Of course, that was a mere beginning. The fairly recent introduction of systematic programing for the almost random efforts at assessment and correction and, what is more important, the use of computer-assisted instruction for aiding, evaluating, and encouraging the individual progress of each student will result, most likely, in as much improvement over the work of the forties and the fifties as the efforts of these years represented an advance over the long centuries that preceded.

Though these are the innovative aspects of the learning of foreign languages, I am less certain about their application to the learning of the earlier stages of one's own language. I should like to find out to what extent our own advanced students of Chaucer, Spenser, or even Shakespeare are learning the language-patterns of these great writers in the manner I have described for foreign languages. You will not be at all shocked by my mention of Chaucer and Spenser — but Shakespeare? Perhaps not to understand the gist of what the Bard had to say, but for a deep, thorough grasp of Shakespeare's meaning, I warmly suggest that a course in Elizabethan English would be a tremendous help, both for vocabulary, and more important, for language structure. And wherever there is to be a course in language, I hold firm to the conviction that a programed course, based on structural linguistic analysis and facilitated by computer-assisted instruction, is a promising method for rapid and thorough learning.

INNOVATIONS IN LEARNING LITERATURE

He who would communicate the messages of our humanistic heritage must first receive them himself from senders who, in turn, have been the recipients of transmittals from the generation before them. In other words, our teachers of English literature, modern foreign languages, or classical literature, in the original or in translation, must themselves have learned two important things: the place of a given masterpiece in the culture from which it sprung, and its relevance to the culture of the present.

Let us consider the first of these. The communicator of the humanities must learn to understand them in the context of their own culture, hence, our specialized courses in literature for those who are to teach it.

What about innovation in this nonlinguistic aspect of literary studies? Can anything about literature be programed and computerized? Can a feeling for Keats's "Ode on a Grecian Urn" be reduced to a predetermined set of questions and answers, with a computer ready to administer the carrot of approval or the stick of rejection to the advancing neophyte? I think not, and I am not even suggesting that it be tried. What can be done and should be done is to reduce to a program all the peripheral facts about the authors and masterpieces of our humanistic heritage and to have the student learn and converse about these with a computer, in his own time and at his own speed. The historical facts about Shakespeare's age, the size, shape, and location of the Globe Theater, conjectures about Shakespeare's parentage, profession, love life, earnings, and the like should probably be known if one is to appreciate his comedies and tragedies to the fullest extent. Surely, they must be known by one who is to teach the plays. So must the well-worn and accepted lines of Shakespearean criticism, if only so the scholar–teacher may be conscious of what he is doing when he departs from them. But does this mean that these items must take up precious minutes of students' and teachers' time when class and instructor are in direct, living contact? I think not.

"What songs the sirens sang," to quote Sir Thomas Browne in *Urn Burial*, "or what name Achilles assumed when he hid himself among women, though puzzling questions . . . ," are the sort of literary trivialities that do not belong to the main effort of the humanistic learning process, whatever other merit they may have. This main effort should be devoted to the fresh understanding of the masterpieces, first in their own terms, and then with relevance to the present. The communicator of the humanities should, himself, be aware of the world in which his students live, so that he may relate the masterpieces of the past to the interests and problems of the present. This means a good foundation for the humanist in social studies.

Innovations in the learning processes of the communicators of our humanistic heritage can, to a lesser extent, be applied to the process of communication itself. All that our high school and beginning college students need to learn about literature, as distinguished from the intrinsic meaning and values of literature itself, should be reduced to programs and administered by computers. Thus, the teacher would be free both to stimulate and to respond to the thoughts of his students in face-to-face contact, once the computer print-out had assured him that the young people knew that Boswell was Sam Johnson's biographer, not Ben Jonson's, that Balboa, and not Cortez, first viewed the Pacific with a wild surmise, that Keats greatly admired Chapman's *Homer*, but that his enthusiasm is not shared by modern critics, and the like.

In addition the tools, as contrasted to the fabric, of literary criticism can be programed. Any self-respecting computer can be taught to distinguish between a metaphor and a simile, to applaud the student who also has learned to do so, and to chide the one who has not, while encouraging the faltering steps of the learner who is on his way to realizing this crucial distinction. Once the technicalities are out of the way, a truly sensitive discussion of the effect of one or the other of these figures of speech in a fine poem can be meaningful and rewarding to learner and teacher alike. Otherwise, in a pedagogical analog to Gresham's Law, the base coinage of the factual, the technical, the readily examinable will drive out of circulation the pure gold of thought, of imagination, and of creation on both sides of the desk. The great innovation we call the Industrial Revolution has transferred to machines much of what, until its advent, men thought had to be done by man alone; what we are here discussing is an extension of that memorable revolution.

INNOVATIONS IN LEARNING FORMAL ENGLISH

A second innovative task for the forward-looking humanist is the task of preserving and, to the extent possible, of strengthening existing modes of intellectual and abstract communication in a manner that is practicable and suitable for our times. I refer now to communication in our own native tongue, English. By the time he is in his teens, if not long before, every native speaker of English of normal intelligence has learned to communicate and to receive communications well enough at the practical level of everyday affairs. This is not to say that every young person who can communicate satisfactorily at the everyday level can function acceptably on the more formal level of standard English. The phenomenon of the poor reader, the poor writer, or the poor speaker at the formal level who is entirely able to communicate in colloquial speech is too well known to require more than mere mention here. H. A. Gleason, Jr., in his *Linguistics and English Gram-*

mar, says of these students: "We have . . . very largely failed to cope adequately with the reading [and, I should add, with the speaking and writing] difficulties of the group not poor enough to warrant remedial work. . . . Their language abilities are rooted in colloquial speech where patterns are comparatively simple, language redundancy is high and generally supplemented by situational redundancy. A rather crude order of skill is sufficient to find meanings with adequate accuracy."

I should like to supplement what Gleason says by adding a conjecture of my own — that the sales promotional patterns of the mass media have led to a greater expectation of and, therefore, a greater dependence on simplicity of construction, redundancy, and repetition than existed before their enormous spread. They have led also to a greater sense of unease when these are lacking.

What of all of this? It is a fact of life and, seemingly, an irreversible one. The maintenance of our gross national product requires promotion of this sort, and we, the beneficiaries of the affluence it produces, should not complain. However, we must be prepared to cope with the consequences of the process. The receivers of these countless messages come to believe that if anyone wants to transmit anything to him, he must do it simply, briefly, and repetitively, with dialogue if possible. Anything else is tricky, complicated, and incomprehensible double-talk.

Let me quote Gleason again as he deals with modern formal prose: "The central parts of the grammatical system are much the same as those the student already knows well. Trouble stems from structural intricacies involving more elaborate combinations of familiar patterns, from more frequent use of patterns rare in speech, and from additional patterns which are probably unfamiliar."

The usual manner in which our schools have tried to cope with the situation Gleason describes is the teaching of grammar. Rules of grammar, often illustrated by copious examples, are taught, and exercises are built around them. However, except for the fact that we are dealing here not with a foreign language but with a separate stratum of the student's native tongue, this procedure differs little from the grammar-translation method now happily being eliminated from our teaching of foreign languages. There the newer methods stress the learning of patterns through practice in transformations, in filling blanks, in answering in the target language questions based on comprehension of sentences employing the patterns under study, and the like — techniques well-adapted to programing and to computer-assisted instruction.

This is all going on in the teaching of modern foreign languages and, surprisingly enough, of Latin. But what of English? Alfred S. Hayes, Director of the Center for Applied Linguistics in Washington, D.C., writes: "The teaching of English to native Americans is still largely based upon medieval notions. We want it to be well taught, but the subject matter has not been sharply defined; there are therefore widely divergent views on how it should be taught. By and large, we have let the teaching of English fall far behind the times, as if we were to tolerate the teaching of alchemy and astrology in our schools instead of modern chemistry and astronomy." If we are to believe Mr. Hayes, and he is an expert in this field, here is surely a fertile ground for innovation.

It is perhaps clear by now what the nature of my proposal for innovation will be. I suggest that we employ pattern-practice, based upon structural linguistic analysis of formal English, as a method of teaching that level of English just as if it were (as it almost is to some native speakers of English) a foreign language, or at least a second language.

Gleason says: "The grammar taught in school has been of very little help in these problems. It deals almost exclusively with patterns with which the student will have little trouble." In a footnote he adds: "There are, of course, some students who do have trouble with some of the central patterns normally included in the grammar syllabus. The majority do not have any RECEPTIVE difficulty, though they may not use these patterns actively."

In the main text, he continues: "To be useful, it [the new grammar] must be extended outward from the central features of the system to the constructions over which the student has inadequate receptive control. What is needed, then, is a grammar that penetrates more deeply into its traditional subject matter, the structure of sentences, so that it can be helpful with the more unusual patterns."

He also calls attention to the importance of transitions used in the tight structure of high quality prose and to the difference between the transitions used in good literary English and those common in good colloquial English. To quote again: "Readers not accustomed to this kind of language have real and troublesome problems here, and this is a place where they need help."

Help in the form of a painstaking analysis of English structure Gleason does indeed give, and his bibliography calls attention to other analyses that have been made recently. This is, of course, only the groundwork for the kind of innovation I have proposed.

If the idea I have proposed should be deemed worthy of action, then an enormously difficult, complex, and time-consuming task lies ahead. A group of scholars (for this would have to be a joint effort) would have to agree upon a structural analysis of formal English prose as a basis. They would then have to select the patterns to be stressed in instruction at various grade levels. These scholars would have to use models selected from the vast corpus of contemporary English writings. The arrangement of all this material so that it could be programed and made the basis of computer-assisted instruction would be another Herculean labor — but the way of the innovator is hard!

If such a system could be put into practice, we might conceivably see a reversal of the trend that virtually makes the teaching of college freshman composition unconstitutional, in the sense that our fundamental code of laws forbids the infliction of "cruel and unusual punishments." That freshman composition falls into this category for a vast number of college instructors of English is known to all their colleagues, and yet the students do not dissent from this stern judgment. The reason for the torture is clear. The instructors know the patterns of expository and narrative English prose; the students, by and large, do not. The instructors have learned these patterns over years of close study and practice, being by self-selection devoted to these matters; the students have diverse and varied interests, and only a small number of them include among these interests a mastery of the features of formal English prose style. But if a course of instruction beginning in the elementary school were to lead them, by slow and graded stages, to a real mastery of the second language that forms a separate stratum of their native tongue, the need for a separate course in expository English composition might effectually be eliminated, and the energies now consumed correcting basic grammatical and stylistic errors might be turned to higher and to better things.

I have treated my two proposals as separate; in a sense they are complementary. If students could be brought, by an innovative treatment of the patterns of formal English prose, to a point of greater receptivity of formal, stylized language in general, they could perhaps more easily be led to an understanding both of masterpieces originally written in English and of those translated into English from foreign languages. If, by the full use of newly developed methods, students were to come into closer and more meaningful contact with the masterpieces of the humanistic tradition, their resistance to learning the patterns of formal English prose might be lessened. Thus, in this period of transition, we might see a new and widespread rejuvenation of humanistic studies, joining linguistic with literary interests, as was fostered by our predecessors in that other great period of transition, the European Renaissance.

Schoolhouse in Transition

Harold B. Gores

A SCHOOL IS THREE THINGS: people, ideas, and a place — in that order of importance. Almost all educators would agree with this simple definition, but most educators, inventive or not, appear totally unaware that the nature and quality of the last component, the place, make a difference worth discussing. However, innovation and invention in the environment of education are proceeding at a pace at least as lively as in the other two sectors.

Innovation, in this area as in any area, is, of course, challenged by those who find security in the status quo, and innovative educators are the natural target of those people. When you are chided for your discontent with how things are in education, take comfort in what Lichtenberg, a 19th-century philosopher, had to say on the subject: "I do not know whether if things change they will get better. But I do know that if they are to get better, they must change." Innovative educators are the voices proclaiming, "Better our customs die than our children," and they are the exceptions to the general rule that everybody wants progress, but nobody wants change.

That nobody wants change necessitates a certain structure or pattern for initiating any desired change. Imagine, for example, that we want to change something about the schoolhouse so that it will be a better place for learning. We already have an idea as to what the change should be. If in our haste to make progress we thrust the change upon those who must make it work, we are likely to discover that the gains we hoped for will never be realized. But if, on the other hand, we ask the people what they want and then we hasten to supply them with all the options, we can safely accept their answer.

Here is a concrete illustration of this. Some years ago we asked the professors at a large university what kind of office space they wanted in a new faculty office building. What they wanted turned out to be what they already had plus 50 square feet. So we started over again, first asking what they wanted and then presenting a series of mock-ups, showing every available option within the state of the art. After the faculty had examined all the options, their response to our original question was supremely intelligent.

Moreover, if the group, given all the options, fails to choose the one you want, the chances are you are wrong. A group of people of good will, possessing all the options as to courses of action, will usually turn out to be smarter than the initiator.

So much for the care and feeding of innovators. What is actually happening to the schoolhouse? What is transpiring is in response to the innovations educators are initiating.

STRUCTURAL CHANGES

Educators are moving education away from the group toward the individual. It has been the national habit to annually cast a net over the young fry, the five-year-olds, sorting them into equal-size boxes called classrooms where, as they grow in size and strength, they leap each June to the next higher box until after 12 leaps they receive a high school diploma. To be sure, the secondary schools, usually being larger than the elementary schools, allow the young to swap boxes on signal during the day. But for all practical purposes, schools are laddered boxes negotiated in a dozen years by about half of our children. A few may make double jumps;

but the vast remaining number, especially in our central cities and in the back country, fail to make the required leaps at the required rate, become discouraged, give up, and leave the boxes altogether.

But here and there the standard groupism is breaking up. The boxes, whether strung along corridors like the coaches of a train or arranged back to back, are crumbling. The walls are coming down; the self-contained, self-contaminating classroom is giving way to large zones of space in which children and teachers are free to work out whatever arrangements seem best to each for the moment, the hour, the day. And, thanks to air conditioning, the schoolhouse need be designed no longer around the winds, which dictate long, narrow fingers, two classrooms wide. Schoolhouses can now be fat and still be comfortable.

Innovative people are also striving to free the child and the teacher from the standard environment in other ways. One such person is Governor Rex Lee of American Samoa. Faced with the need to build 23 elementary schools, he came to us for help. He had noticed that as a device for social change, educating the young is a slow process. It takes a generation of educating the young before they come into the management of their society. He saw at once that unless he educated the adults, while educating the children, the society could collapse before the educated children inherited it. So his question was: "How do we design schools that will not only teach the young but simultaneously teach adults?" This is the kind of question that some of our beleaguered central cities should be asking.

Governor Lee also had some ideas about schools. He asked whether schools could be designed to leave the small child on the floor, not propped up in a slippery plastic chair locked to a plastic-topped desk. He had found small Samoan children on the floor, where all small children prefer to be, and he wanted to leave them there. Not until the secondary school would he force the child to sit in a chair, thus preparing him for college in the United States where people sit in chairs. He concluded that the American coffee table, about 15 inches high, was the ideal desk if the child worked off the floor. Rex Lee then saw clearly that by leaving the young in their natural habitat, the floor, he could design elementary schools that would serve better both the children and the adults.

A kindergarten teacher in Oklahoma City, Peggy Loeffler, is another environmental innovator. She wanted to build an early childhood center that would provide the equivalent of the environment surrounding a teacher and her class walking in the woods on the finest day of June. In such a school, she said, the teacher would gather the children around her, as in the forest, and the children would be sitting on logs, hummocks, moss, ledges, rocks, on whatever nature provides. In short, Mrs. Loeffler's school for young children would be an acre of June. To create such a school is well within our technical capability. The frontier is not architecture but education.

Consider the complaint of one of the manufacturers of partitions. He was dismayed that we seemed to be encouraging the idea that the interior of a school might have no walls at all. My answer to him was that the egg-crate arrangement of standard classrooms will continue to be the dominant pattern in schools for another generation; however, if he would like to court the business of school districts that are making the transition from 19th-century forms to 20th-century forms, he should work on a successor to the partition.

He should think of a large zone of space as a pond in which the ducks — the teachers — and the ducklings — the children — swim about in the course of the day. Moored against the bank of the room would be "sails," literally sail-like partitions that, on demand, could be floated across the space to constitute classrooms as required. Some of the sails could be multicolored, and some could contain kangaroo pouches for storage. In such a mutable, malleable, flexible environment, teachers could constitute and reconstitute instant classrooms by sailing up walls whenever visual privacy was required.

Already we see this concept emerging in the great ponds of space the Granada School in California provides in its hexagonal pods.

Improving Interior Comfort

In these structural ways, educators are indeed moving away from the group toward the individual. Educators are also moving education away from puritan austerity toward 20th-century efficiency. Until very recently, schools in northern latitudes were designed to keep children warm; in southern latitudes, they were designed to keep children dry. None were designed to keep children comfortable. Yet, without legislation, children are winning a new right. In the old days, until the 1950's, children clearly had the right not to be cold. In the 1960's, children won the right not to be hot. Any school today contemplating usefulness the year round will, at any latitude, provide cooling as well as heating. Dr. Johnson, Medical Director of New York's Life Extension Institute, says that productivity of office workers can be affected by as much as 15 per cent by the quality of environment. We can safely generalize that productivity in school is similarly affected; and 15 per cent is good interest on your money.

It seems reasonable too that if a child can hear better and his teacher is less fatigued, more learning will take place. This suggests that the reverberative, ceramic, masonry box in which we encapsulate teacher and class be softened at least to the extent of making the floor acoustically absorbent. In the past our classrooms have been like kitchens — kitchen floor, masonry walls, factory lights, unyielding furniture of iron and plastic — the whole arrangement made tolerable by the only thing in the room that could yield to the touch but is beyond reach, the acoustic ceiling.

Current educators have insisted that the child be able to hear better, see better, and feel better; and so the classroom has changed. It's being tipped upside down; now the acoustic surface is on the floor where an older culture, the Oriental, has always known it belongs. In 1954, despite the fact that there are 100,000 acres of school floors in the United States, the total sale of carpeting was $50,000. Last year, the sale of carpeting for schools amounted to $99 million and outranked sales to hotels, motels, theatres, and all the other institutional consumers of carpeting. The echo-cavern schools, so admired by nuts-and-bolts maintenance departments, are giving way to more humane and functional arrangements.

Considering this reference to money, we must remember to put all school building costs in their proper perspective. A new million-dollar high school building will require an operating budget of about one million dollars every three years. If we impute to the building a life of 60 years, the cost of the original building itself over that period is only five per cent of the total cost of fulfilling the purposes and the programs that prompted its construction in the first place.

In other words, every time a school board adds two teachers, it has taken an act that over 30 years is the fiscal equivalent of building a million-dollar schoolhouse. If this be true, it is hard to understand how school boards can devote brief discussion to additional personnel and spend the rest of the night arguing about how to cheapen the construction of an addition to an elementary school. If quality of environment can make a 15 per cent difference in the productivity of the other 95 per cent that is spent after the building is built, it is simple prudence to build well in the beginning.

Today many schools throughout the country exhibit this virtue. The Granada School in California is one. It provides large ponds — really large ponds — of space in which the faculty are free to redesign the school hour by hour. Another is Barrington Middle School in Illinois where, by taking advantage of the most modern industrial design, the school is free to reshape itself as new teacher–pupil arrangements emerge. P.S. 219 in New York City is a great zone of free space under a dome, that R. Buckminster Fuller calls, "a scoop of the sky."

This New York City school is the best example of open space in the country — not an acre of June, to be sure, but a quarter of an acre.

A secondary school in Clarksville, Tennessee, provides great zones of comfortable (air conditioned), quiet (carpeted), flexible (few partitions) space, enabling the school to move toward individual instruction as rapidly as the faculty can manage it. In Cleveland an abandoned warehouse became a Supplementary Education Center — an exciting new art form in education. This warehouse was made educationally livable by the treatment of its interiors. Finally, there will be in Harlem an academy that may lead the way to better space, more quickly erected, in the so-called core city. A 10,000-square-foot, air-conditioned supermarket will be converted to school space.

It may well be that through these conversions of commercial buildings, as in Cleveland and New York, we may eventually receive public consent to create humane, living room interiors in the conventional schoolhouse. Strangely we seem to make greater progress in creating good learning environments if the building is not something called a "schoolhouse." There is something about the word "schoolhouse" that locks a municipality into a train of thought that produces only great masonry fortresses, afloat on a sea of blacktop, but, if the school is converted from some other use, we are free to treat its interiors as though children were people.

TRADITIONAL CONCEPTS ARE CHANGING

Thus, the old ways of doing things are gradually eroding. Even the old formulas are being questioned — for example, the notion that the school site must be 20 acres plus an acre for every hundred children. In the central city, such a formula would wipe out the homes of the student body. Thanks to new products coming on the market like synthetic turfs, good schools can be built on limited sites, and the rule of thumb that has dictated that schools of less than 750 pupils are inefficient and that schools of larger than 1,250 are necessarily impersonal is being questioned. Today we know that a school can be as large as it has to be and still be a good school, provided that administrative organization is altered. If administrative organization remains monolithic, 1,250 pupils is probably a valid maximum, but reorganization into subschools, as at Evanston and Newton, indicates that the size of a school is primarily a matter of logistics.

Even the presumed life of a school is being reexamined. Already there are schools being planned with an eye toward their conversion to some other purpose in the future. In the past the schoolhouse has been good for little else. Only if we build well, will the schoolhouse convert to another useful purpose.

Indeed, the whole notion of the separate schoolhouse is being challenged in the central city. New York, Philadelphia, and Chicago are moving rapidly toward joint occupancy — the sharing of school facilities with such compatible partners as housing, business, and light manufacturing. The New York City Educational Construction Fund envisions the use of education to key the redesigning of neighborhoods. Pittsburgh and New Haven are also employing education to key the city's renewal, and Syracuse will be reestablishing elementary education in four great schools located on the city's periphery, thus leading to the abandonment of the downtown schools. Educators should encourage these central cities as they look toward their suburbs for ways of creating metropolitan districts.

This then is the present scene in educational environment, a scene where educators are finally creating schools for individuals. Educators have special responsibility to come up with the ideas, the innovations, and the inventions that such creation requires. Inventive individuals can influence schools to use Title III funds imaginatively and constructively, so that R & D will indeed signify Research and Development, as it does in business and industry, instead of signifying, as it has so often in education, Retirement and Death.

Education and Societal Needs

Overviews

BLACKBOARD POWER

James Farmer

The "magnolia myth" image of Negroes as happy slaves strumming guitars under magnolia trees still exists in American education. It must be destroyed, for people cannot elevate themselves if this kind of self-image is presented to them. The right kind of education — integrated and of superior quality — is the key to the elevation of Negroes in American society. However, until this is accomplished on a large scale existing ghetto schools must provide education that is superior in quality to that provided in middle-class white schools to compensate for the difficulties minority group children face in learning.

Current instructional materials are not relevant to the expression and needs of ghetto children. Negroes must be able to learn of the development of the Negro subculture — music, dance, literature, and history — and of Negro contributions to American history and society. Furthermore, teachers in the ghettos must become sensitive to the environment from which the children come. The whole community must be enabled to take part, through neighborhood school boards and indigenous school aides, in the exciting adventure of education. If the community participates, the school will be not merely in but of that community and, as such, will truly be a key to elevation and a sense of personal dignity.

CURRENT PATTERNS OF GENERATIONAL CONFLICT

Edgar Z. Friedenberg

"If you dig the music, you will dig the youngsters." Any adult who wants to receive a relatively complete message across the generation gap must learn to listen to the music of young people and will probably enjoy doing so. Bob Dylan and the Beatles do have something to say; they are speaking eloquently of the patterns of generational conflict in which young people are so involved.

The generational conflict today, as represented by the hippie movement, is something more fundamental than the usual conflict between generations, for it is a rejection of the very basis of our society — the goals and ideals of the middle class. The development of the hippies' subculture is an effort to strengthen their avoidance of socialization; the use of drugs has only intensified the eternal conflict between individuals whose sense of personal security is derived chiefly from reliance on order and control and those who feel safest when they are in close touch with their feelings but are perpetually threatened by repression and restraint.

How any adult responds to this conflict depends fundamentally upon his view of its legitimacy — whether he feels that this is a problem that must be treated by repression or whether he believes that meaningful changes in social institutions are necessary.

Blackboard Power

James Farmer

CREATIVE CHANGE in education is the most vital issue in America today. There is no other issue in which the lives of people — men, women, and children — hang so much in the balance. This is a time of great crisis in our nation and cities — a time of tremendous turmoil and change. Changes are taking place in the mood and attitude of poor people, especially the black poor throughout the country. Today the masses of Negro citizens are coming to the conclusion that education is the key, if there is any one key, to the elevation of their status in American society.

Educators and school administrators have a weighty burden resting upon their shoulders. We have failed, all of us, and this failure is not yours any more than it is mine. The failure is that of our entire system, which has not succeeded in educating the poor children in our nation. These children are suffering from a syndrome of poverty and prejudice, and poor education and functional illiteracy are serving as a foundation for that syndrome.

In seeking to solve this fundamental problem, Negroes are approaching it in two different ways: (1) through the goal of integrated schools, and (2) through the goal of high quality education in ghetto schools. Since American leaders have not succeeded in desegregating education, many Negroes, especially the militants, are turning away from the concept of integrated schools. Their main interest is in the quality of education their children receive. They say they do not want integration and philosophically claim that the Negro needs more identity and equality, especially through the development of his own sub-culture — music, dance, literature, and history. They believe that Negroes cannot become educated through integrated schools. This belief has resulted from the failure of the integration effort and the new emphasis upon identity and self-expression, which is now the major thrust in the Civil Rights movement.

If you must categorize me, I am something of a synthesist, for I believe that integration and high quality ghetto education must somehow be combined. At the time of the Supreme Court Decision in 1954, most of us had a dispersionist theory of integration. Liberal people then believed that the ghettos were going to cease to exist, that Harlem would disappear. All this, obviously, was nonsense.

In those days, no responsible Negro leader would have proposed improving the school facilities or housing in a Harlem, for example, or a Watts. He would have been condemned as perpetuating segregation. It was felt then that Negroes would have no identity and would disappear as a group.

This view was a kind of self-abnegation and was unrealistic. The Harlems of our country are going to continue to exist. They will exist long after we have achieved open occupancy housing. Even after that is achieved, many Negroes will choose to live in what is now Harlem or Watts or the Hawk district of Cleveland or the black ghettos of other cities. Some will choose to live there because it is home. Their roots, such as they are, have grown from that soil. Others will live there because they have no capital to uproot themselves and move.

We also must face the fact that in most of our cities it is becoming increasingly difficult to have integration according to the 50 per cent guidelines of the U.S. Office of Education. In Washington, D.C., for example, 93 per cent of the school population is black. It is frankly not possible to have schools throughout that city contain less than 50 per cent Negroes. In most of our other cities where there is a substantial Negro, Puerto Rican, or Mexican-American population, we are approaching that same point. Obviously we cannot achieve complete desegregation.

However, we must achieve as much integration as we possibly can because there is virtue in integration. It is in itself an important educational value. Our children, black and white, must learn to live with people who look different from themselves, talk differently, dress differently, and come from different cultures. Otherwise we are not training them to live in today's world.

At the same time we must recognize that many of the schools will be predominantly Negro in the foreseeable future. Therefore, we must provide higher quality education in those schools — not equal education, but superior education because of the difficulties these children face in learning.

As we seek to provide both high quality education and integrated education, what are the problems confronting us?

CURRICULUM AND MATERIALS TO IMPROVE SELF-IMAGE

One important problem stems from the fact that education, in the past and indeed in the present, is geared far too largely to the needs of white middle-class children and not to the needs of the deprived. Actually the term *culturally deprived* is a misnomer. Rather we should refer to these people as *culturally deviant,* because they do possess cultures, though they are different. Indeed their cultures often are very rich with elements that can be extremely beneficial.

Nevertheless, there are a number of reasons why it is difficult for the children from so-called deprived families to learn. One is that many of our schools are more interested in teaching them than in having children learn. It is not enough for education to be placed before children. The responsibility of the school goes much further than that. The schools — their administrators and their teachers — must assure that the children learn and seek solutions when they do not. If they do not learn, the schools have not done their job.

It has been pointed out by Daniel P. Monahan and others that the home background of many of the children from deprived communities is such that learning becomes difficult. Monahan refers to the matriarchy of the Negro family, especially the poor Negro family, and to the lack of books, magazines, and newspapers in the home. Obviously if parents have not been educated, it becomes more difficult for their children to achieve academically. But to say that since the homes have not been adequate to prepare the children for education and we, therefore, cannot teach them is to indulge in a giant and class dropout. It is our responsibility to teach them in spite of everything.

Another problem is that materials used in so many of the city schools attended by Negro children and other minority group children are not relevant to their lives and circumstances. The fact is they must learn about themselves. If one does not know anything about himself, he has no real reason to learn about anything. What a person learns must relate to himself and his environment.

Therefore, the curricula should be decentralized so that the curriculum in a given school would be relevant to the needs of the people in that community. An Indian on a reservation does not need to know about Wall Street financing when he studies economics. This is not important to him. Similarly a Negro in the ghetto, if he studies economics, needs to know about business in Harlem — the bad balance of payments there, with dollars going out and not coming in, with no production of goods and services. This is what he needs to know rather than high finance on Wall Street.

Even more important, the Negro must be able to study his contributions to America. At present Negroes do not study about themselves — about Negro history and its contributions to that of the nation. This is one of the prime emphases of the whole Civil Rights movement at the present time — the necessity for an identity on the part of people. One of the tragedies in Negro life in our country is that the Negro is not identified with the development of his own very rich subculture.

Identification, then is one of the most crucial concerns facing the Negro, for he does not, at this point, have an acceptable self-image. In most history books, either there is no mention of the contributions of Negroes or a stereotyped image is presented. What is this stereotyped image? Is it the "magnolia myth" — Negroes as happy and contented slaves who fitted admirably into the slave institution and thrived upon the paternalistic care of the slave owner — Negroes who loved slavery, who sat under the magnolia trees strumming their guitars and singing sweetly of the hereafter.

That is the kind of image that has been presented. The textbooks in Washington, D.C., for example, present that image in spite of the fact that the school population is 93 per cent Negro. What dignity and self-respect can a child develop from such a presentation? In one textbook used in Washington, there are illustrations showing Negro children "what a Negro is." One picture presents a cotton field in which slaves with toothy grins and big protruding eyes are wearing bandannas, chopping cotton, and having a wonderful time.

This has been a travesty, and it does not end with the public schools. It goes on through college. A number of years ago at Reed College in Portland, Oregon, I met with seniors who were history majors. Not a single one of them knew that 100,000 Negroes fought on the Union side in the Civil War. None of them knew that slave revolts had rocked the land, and none had heard of Negro leaders like Nat Turner, Denmark Vesey, or Gabriel Prosser. They too held the "magnolia myth" image.

There must be an inclusion of Negro history and the contributions of Negroes to American history in the curriculum. The materials that the Negro studies must relate to his life and his experiences. If one has no history, then one has no future. If one has no past, one is nothing. It is the responsibility of our schools to change the adverse self-image Negroes have.

MORE AND BETTER TEACHERS

This is only one reason for the difficulties these children have in learning. Another is overcrowded schools that have a bad pupil-teacher ratio, with sometimes double-shift classes and, occasionally, triple-shift classes. Teachers in such circumstances are merely policemen trying to maintain order.

Studies of several schools in big cities indicated that teachers spent 80 per cent of their time on nonteaching duties. To help remedy such situations, we must lighten the class load of the teacher and make more adequate use of teachers' aides and assistants who are indigenous — those who know the community, who are familiar with the experiences of the children and who, therefore, can relate to them.

The attitude of the teacher may indeed be crucial. If the teacher — white or black — does not believe in the capacity of the children he seeks to teach, that teacher has foreclosed on the possibility of teaching them. I heard one Harlem teacher, who was not white but black, remark to two other teachers, "Why do you sweat? You are not training kids to go to Harvard."

Ghetto children quickly develop "high sensitivity antennas." They know who are their friends and who are their enemies, and they sense very quickly the attitude of the person with whom they are dealing. If a teacher stands before them with the attitude that they cannot learn, those children will erect a barrier because that teacher has said to them precisely what society has said to them — that they are of no worth. To some extent they have come to believe it themselves.

Inservice and preservice training of teachers is, therefore, of tremendous importance. Teachers must be trained in human relations and, more important, they must become sensitive to the environment from which the children come. They must learn rapidly about the homes and the families of these children and of the problems these children have so they can deal effectively with them.

Also these children need some Negro males to educate them and to administer their education. This is extremely important for the development of a good self-image. Negro children have always seen black people following orders, not giving them, and holding subservient positions rather than decision-making or policy-making positions. This situation must be changed.

COMMUNITY AND PARENT PARTICIPATION

More opportunities for active community–parent involvement in education must also be developed. For a long time parents of deprived children looked upon educators and the schools as being a part of officialdom, an island isolated from the affairs of the community. This was a tragic turn of mind, but it existed. The Negro mother and father who lived in Harlem feared officialdom because their experience, and the experience of their parents, had been that officialdom served to further the oppressor. Therefore, they stayed away from the schools. Now that attitude is changing.

These parents realize that education is the key to their elevation in society, and they want to participate in the exciting adventure of education. We must not leave them out. We must consider decentralizing school boards in order to set up the machinery for community and parent participation in community school boards or neighborhood school boards. These parents may not know how to develop the curriculum most effectively, but they can tell you what they want their children to learn about themselves; they may not understand the process of learning, but they have something of great value to contribute — a burning, passionate interest in the future of their children. Moreover, they have a knowledge and immediate acquaintanceship with the community from which these children come and with the problems of that community. We must hear them or lose a vital element for progress.

No program or innovation in our schools can succeed unless we involve the parents and the community in the process of education and unless we relate that education to the experiences and the needs of that community. I urge you to become a part of this whole revolution. I urge you to become part of it because it is not only for little children whose skins are black or who speak Spanish; it is for all of us — white and black, North and South. It is for the nation. This nation cannot survive, split as it is, with polarization increasing almost by the day between the races. The tensions are growing and becoming worse. The way to relieve them is by tackling their causes. Their causes are economic and they are social, but fundamentally they are educational. Their solution lies in our sense of humanity, a quality that transcends blackness and whiteness. That sense of humanity must be developed, communicated, and preserved if we are to succeed in this most important of endeavors. In the words of Hillel, the great rabbi who wrote some 2,000 years ago: "If I am not for myself, who will be for me? If I am for myself alone, what am I? And if not now, when?"

Current Patterns of Generational Conflict

Edgar Z. Friedenberg

ARE THE CONFRONTATIONS between young people and their elders that so pervade our life today seriously different in kind from those characteristic of the past? The answer to this question, which concerns most discussions of current generational conflict, is, "Very different indeed."

TRADITIONAL CONFLICTS

There are, of course, many different kinds of intergenerational conflict, and the kinds that have become traditional still occur today. Most conflicts between young and old are still clashes over specific issues that reflect no special discontent with society as such; many of those encounters that do reflect social discontent, however, continue to use rather familiar political ideas and postures to express it. Neither clashes with authority nor political protests are, as such, novel. But the major reason why there is so much interest in the question today is precisely because we rather generally sense that many young dissenters reject society in a new and much more fundamental way. To paraphrase Bob Dylan slightly, "Mr. Jones does indeed know that something is happening; and if he doesn't know what it is, he would like to find out."

How large a proportion of contemporary youth is seriously

disaffected is an open question but not a very important one. The magnitude varies, and what the disaffection means is more important than how widespread it may be. Moreoever, by becoming preoccupied with the number of people who raise an issue, we avoid facing the issue they raise. This evasion has become conventional in our society, and in itself affords an excellent example of the quantitative approach to life that "turns off" disaffected youth.

In our own earlier conflicts with our elders, we most frequently felt that we had become more nearly equal, if not superior, to them than they would admit and that we were being denied the opportunity to use skills and fill social roles. We fought them for the right to do what they were doing and to prove that we could do as well or better. Such intergenerational conflict still goes on today between "square" but ambitious and impatient young people and their elders, whose life styles they accept as examples of those that exist and among which they must ultimately choose.

This still is probably the commonest, though no longer the most important, kind of intergenerational conflict. For our generation the claims of the young who merely wish to replace us and prove that they can do better are hardly threatening. This sort of conflict has been thoroughly institutionalized in traditional "sandbox" student government and in bureaucratic procedures by which the educational system itself provides for promotion and graded success of failure. Far from being a threat to the socialization of the young, we depend on it to provide the motivation for socialization. It is precisely in seeking to defeat their elders at their own game that youth is willing to play and thus insure that the game will continue.

DISAFFECTIONS OF HIPPIES

But there are many young people identified as hippies whose conflict with us concerns much more profound issues than the question of whether they should be in the driver's seat. It would be a better use of metaphor to suggest that they feel as if they were locked in the back of a vehicle that had been built on corrupt specifications, was unsafe at any speed, and was being driven by a middle-aged drunk. They don't want to drive, they don't even want to go where the car is going, and they sometimes distrust the examiners too much even to be willing to apply for a license. What they want is to get out while they are still alive; if they succeed in that, they will try to camp where they happen to be, hoping to make it if they can stay together, and will leave ambition and the Great Society to us.

This attitude is a real threat to social continuity, especially to that of the middle class and its way of life. This kind of disaffection occurs almost exclusively among middle-class or formerly middle-class youth. Few hippies originate in the working or lower classes; members of these classes are usually hostile to hippies when they encounter each other on the urban scene. It is true that lower-class youth, especially Negro youth, has also come to express great disaffection and to express it more violently than in the past. But conflict between lower-class youth and the authority of their elders still basically follows the traditional pattern, which hippie middle-class youth is abandoning. Lower-class youngsters protest the lack of opportunities that keep them down — poor and scanty job openings, restrictive and humiliating school routines, systems of grading that discriminate against them through biases that are built into the very cognitive style of the school and its testing routines, and police surveillance that degrades them and leaves them with arrest records that bar them from employment, even if no charge against them has ever been sustained. These are real and serious grievances, but the effort to redress them does not threaten official social values, which affirm that discrimination is evil and support the demand for improved and equalized opportunity.

The demands of lower-status youth support and validate the basic values of our society because, in protesting against discrimination, they assert their faith in the value of what is withheld from them and their resentment at being deprived of it. This is true even when their protest is violent and disruptive. The looters who sacked Watts in the course of the riots carried off whiskey and portable TV's. What better evidence could they have provided of their fidelity to our common cultural heritage? But hippie youth are, though nonviolent, far more deeply disaffected. They dislike alcohol and resent the tolerance accorded alcoholism by a society that continually harasses them, and may even imprison them as felons, for using marijuana, which is a much less messy drug in its effects and a safer one physiologically. While they may carry a transistor tuned esoterically to the local rock station, their basic attitude toward the media is better expressed in the second endpaper of the album, *Absolutely Free,* of the highly expressive rock group, The Mothers of Invention. Taking the form of a parody of a protest poster, it bears a hideous photograph of the most sinister looking of the "Mothers," all of whom are men, and the exhortation, "Kill Ugly Radio!"

Neither the extent nor the intensity of hippie rejection of our society can be estimated from observing the more dramatic and publicized enclaves like San Francisco's Haight-Ashbury, which is already, like Greenwich Village before it, a tourist trap abandoned by its devotees as a polluted area. Perhaps most middle-class youngsters are still fundamentally "square." However, their squareness is costing them status and respect among the community of youth, and conventional young people are apt to develop some disturbing behaviors of their own when they find that their conventionality no longer earns them the rewards they believed were implicitly guaranteed by their social contact with the establishment. Even class presidents and cheerleaders become unnerved as their peers "turn on" and drop out of the high schools' officially creditable activities. Scattered observation rather consistently suggests that the traditional age gradient for diffusion of deliquent practices has largely been reversed. It is the younger adolescents now who are likely to introduce their curious, but relatively "up-tight" older peers to acid or, in the case of an unusually sheltered older adolescent, even pot.

Whatever the proportion of squares to hippies to be found in any adolescent group, it is certainly clear that the norms have shifted in favor of the hippie life style. It should be equally clear that this is no victory for amorality. It is the hippies and teeny-boppers (very young hippies) who assert the importance of moral behavior and who either actively condemn and protest the immorality of the society that surrounds them or regard their own commitment to "love, flowers, and music" as an implicit act of condemnation. In their comments on "plastic" people and their "plastic" society, they sound very much like an old-fashioned British judge pronouncing a sentence of death on a murderer — very gentle, resolute, detached, and convinced that, considering his character, the man could hardly have hoped to come to a better end. Is this love? Perhaps. It is certainly kinder than being nibbled to death by social workers.

These young people are very firmly convinced that they will never become like their elders, and they are willing to make the most extreme sacrifices of comfort and security to avoid this fate. They are willing to go to jail rather than fight in the Viet Nam war and to live in squalor rather than acquire the credentials our society demands of those whom it rewards with middle-class amenities. Will they persist in so stark a choice as they grow older and less energetic and face the decline of their sustaining sense of community as less committed members defect? Juvenile delinquents do not. When they outgrow their social roles, they usually abandon their delinquent behavior and pass anonymously into the ordinary life of their social class, usually having lost the opportunity to become professional criminals. Organized crime recruits as cautiously as any Madison Avenue firm and tends to reject youths whose clumsiness or impulsiveness has left them with criminal records. None of our relentless and ingenious programs for socializing juvenile delinquents has proved successful, and none has proved necessary. The life of crime has become bureaucratized and rejects them whether or not they reject it, leaving most to choose among the less rewarding legitimate alternatives still available to persons who have made poor use of their opportunity to become trained.

The same thing may happen to hippies as they grow older, but I doubt it. Their values are much less like those that prevail in the larger society than are those of juvenile delinquents. A person who is genuinely committed to openness, feeling, self-expression, and to the use of those drugs which, in his experience, contribute to these and who really abhors violence and prefers squalor to ornate vulgarity may resist conventional efforts to socialize him even over the long haul. Most of the hippier young people I know do not even regard this as an exercise of will. They could not, they feel, become like their parents or most of their teachers or employers even by an act of will. They might if, like their elders, they regarded their emotions as a possession — a set of tools to be used in pursuit of practical ends and overhauled by therapy when they give trouble. But this is just what they don't do.

How can one account for the hippies' devotion to feeling and responsiveness and to their relatively durable resistance to socialization? There are no firm answers to these questions. The youngsters I am discussing are very different from Keniston's *Uncommitted;* they have not been subjected to and probably would not cooperate in any comparable study.

DEVELOPMENT OF YOUTH SUBCULTURE

It is quite likely that their more savage right-wing critics are correct in at least one particular — the more permissive child-rearing practices of the past 20 years seem, despite many conspicuous and silly abuses, to be paying off as promised in greater emotional freedom and a deeper sense of selfhood. Moreover, hippie youth has finally begun to develop what

James S. Coloman and others have attributed, I think prematurely, to their more conventional peers — a real subculture of adolescents and young adults with its own values, its own relatively independent status system, and its own art in the form of posters, buttons, and, of course, music. This culture even has its own press, like the San Francisco *Oracle*, the Los Angeles *Free Press*, Berkeley *Barb*, and the East Lansing (Michigan) *Paper*. Most notable are the growing number of underground newspapers published by high school students who face suspension if they distribute them on campus, and harassment by their school administrations in any case. What is most remarkable about these papers is the fact that the level of literary expression achieved in them, and punished by school authorities as irresponsible or obscene where possible, is very high, while at the same time, and often in the same schools, there is an unavailing struggle to teach students to read and write within the limits acceptable to the social system that controls the schools.

This subculture is not, of course, independent of the larger culture that opposes it and to which it is vulnerable. However, its young members are not so vulnerable as they would be without it. They can sustain each other emotionally, hide and nurture fugitives from the adult world, and validate one another's experiences and personal worth. Between these young people and the middle-aged middle class, there is not only a barrier to communication or a generation gap, there is a real conflict of interest. The institutions that we justify as necessary to their socialization, like the schools and the juvenile courts, with their ancillary control apparatus of attendance teachers, and parole officers with their extensive powers of detention, appear to them like the forces a colonial power directs against a native population, justifying the coercive destruction of their preferred way of life as a benevolent effort to raise their level of sanitation, improve their standard of living, and increase their economic opportunity by training them to work usefully and willingly in the conqueror's fields and factories.

LEGAL AND SOCIAL CONSTRAINTS ON YOUTH

Youth in America is, indeed, subjected to a measure of coercion that no other element of the population, even adult Alabama Negroes, must accept. No one else is controlled by special courts that operate from the legal presumption that their intervention into the respondent's affairs is always undertaken *in the respondent's own interest* and is, therefore, by nature impunitive, so that no provision need be made for a formal defense or for formal charges that a law has been violated. Juvenile authorities can and do intervene in the lives of youngsters presumed to be potential delinquents; they pride themselves on taking into account reports on the adjudicated youngster's character, attitude, and general conduct as well as legal evidence, for their purpose is not to punish but to prescribe a remedial regimen. Since the decision of the U.S. Supreme Court in the Galt case last year, juvenile courts are now required to provide most of the formal constitutional safeguards to which adults are entitled to youngsters who are in fact charged with serious violations of the criminal code. Such formal proceedings, however, are but a small part of the court's usual business. Essentially the courts are a socializing apparatus, authorized to intervene if youth, by the standards of the community, is irresponsible or taking a wrong turn.

Youth, moreover, is subject to many other forms of legal coercion from which adults are free: curfew laws, loitering laws, and special laws governing motor vehicle operation, public assembly, dancing, and, of course, drinking. The function, if not the stated purpose, of those laws is quite clearly to reduce the scope of personal autonomy and, with it, the opportunity of young people for diversity in growth or, in their own term, to "do their own thing." The most massive sources of constraint — so big they are nearly invisible — are the school attendance laws and, for young men, the Selective Service Act. All these constraints reinforce each other. It is perfectly possible for a young man to lose his life in Viet Nam without ever having enjoyed the freedom to decide how long he would wear his hair, or to belong to an organization that could invite anyone it wished to address it, or to refuse to allow his locker or his living quarters to be searched without a warrant, or even to walk the streets as late as he wished.

None of this sounds very new, but school-leaving ages have been and are progressively rising; only the escalation of the Viet Nam war has made the draft a real fact of life for middle-class youth. The pressures are greater now then they were, and are growing. Nevertheless, they seem justified to many adults, and even to many young people, who assume that the socialization of the young into the dominant society and the obligation of the young to accept its authority and perform its military missions is inherently necessary and legitimate, and that this legitimacy cannot be placed in doubt by attacking the legitimacy of the social order itself. From this point of view, hippie, dissenting youth are at best a social problem and at worse a public menace. If society is to be preserved, the generation gap must be bridged and a bridgehead established from which to invade and capture, or heartily seduce, the recalcitrant young. To the recalcitrant young themselves, the efforts of society to constrain them and put them to use seem obviously illegitimate because the society itself is seen as illegitimate; the fact that it utilizes the law in its attempts does not make them any more legitimate. It merely means that moral people must learn to accept the necessity of going to jail, as has often enough been necessary in the past.

How any adult will respond to the challenge of alienated youth depends fundamentally on his view of this current crisis in legitimacy. The conventional response is to assume that since civilization must always frustrate the instinctual drives of its members, they cannot cite their frustration as justification for dropping out of it; their alienation must be treated as a social or psychological problem. What you then do depends upon how you respond to social problems. Some have stated that they favor a "carrot-and-stick" policy for motivating recalcitrant youth. More sophisticated operators, some of whom would willingly be just as punitive if they thought punishment would work, try more manipulative approaches to involve youth again. Many, perhaps most, experimental high school and college programs seem designed to break the institution into smaller and more intense groups; they require more student participation without actually sharing any decision-making power or facing the real bases of the students' disaffection. While this is manipulation, it is, nevertheless, often sincerely liberal in intent. The program is based on the premise that even the most disaffected share an obligation to respect the outcome of any political process in which they have been induced to participate; if, in fact, their participation has been powerless, they are still obligated to be realistic about *that*.

Since, however, it is the political and social structure that hippie youth distrusts, on the basis of its fruits as they know them, liberalism does not, to understate the case, turn them on. A more promising basis of rapproachement is to be found in what seem to me to be genuine social responses to at least some of the issues raised by these young people and their plight in society. A particularly clear indication of the kind of thing I find more hopeful is the little publicized decision handed down in April 1967 in New York City by Federal Judge Constance Baker Motley in *Maderas vs Board of Education*. The decision states that a child and his parents may have legal representation at a hearing that may result in the child's suspension from school. The Board, and even *The New York Times* in a subsequent editorial, opposed the decision as opening the way for legal intervention into the internal affairs of the schools. But Judge Motley based her decision not on young Victor Maderas' specific complaint but on the fact that such administrative hearings may lead to the incarceration of a child in an institution no less local for being called a "special" or "residential school" and that statements made by the child or his parents at such hearings may, subsequently, be used in criminal actions against them for truancy or contributing to the delinquency of a minor. This decision in a lower court may well contribute more to establishing the rights of youth on a day-to-day basis than the Supreme Court decision in the Galt case, though this provides some real recognition that even minors possess enough inherent dignity to be entitled to constitutional protection. The consternation with which this decision was received by many juvenile authorities is evidence enough that it really does mean something.

Less hopeful, however, have been the comments of certain justices in their recent decisions upsetting obscenity convictions. These justices have indicated that they would look with contrasting favor on laws designed to forbid the distribution to minors of possibly pornographic books to which adults had a right of access. The whole question of pornography has been dealt with in terms designed to reduce social conflict rather than to clarify the issues involved. It is precisely a work which recognizes the richness and variety of the possible relationships of sexuality to feeling and personal communion that is likely to validate the process of growing up and free young people from some of their hang-ups and alienation; flat textbook descriptions of sexual apparatus and behavior, which are generally regarded as suitable to minors, are either meaningless or, by design, alienating.

All the constraints and restrictions on youth that I have discussed are alienating; that is, their function for socialization is alienating. Socialization may best be defined as the systematic extinction of alternatives, the reduction of the potentially unassimilable view of disruptive thought to the level of the literally unthinkable. Socialization also emphasizes a complementary function — indoctrination — or as we more frequently choose to call it, "transmitting our cultural heritage," that is, communicating to the young what may be thought or must be thought and what alternatives society will plan and even encourage. Education, in a period of little conviction, seems to consist primarily in communicating just this information. It does not seek to convince but it seeks to indicate subtly, but clearly, which interpretations of reality will be tolerated. The network TV programs on the *Warren Report,* which stimulated confidence in it without seeking to meet responsible criticism, provide the best possible example of the process. Both repression and indoctrination work toward the same end — increased social stability on terms set by those currently in power and consistent with the moral tradition they endorse, at the cost of alienating us from those of our feelings and insights that might impede the process.

This, basically, is what hippie youth will no longer accept, and this, too, explains their peculiar choice in drugs. Acid and pot — LSD and marijuana — share, though unequally, the power to restore to some extent the balance in the eternal struggle between perception, not just sensation, and cognition as contributors to our view of reality. While I prefer a balanced view, achieved without chemical intervention, that makes full use of both cognition and feeling, it is surely evident that this struggle has been biased in the favor of cognition since the time of Descartes and that a shift in the point of equilibrium is overdue. *Cogito, ergo sum* is an impressive statement, but in the days of McNamara and Herman Kahn, both exceptionally intelligent men, one is justified in responding, "But oh, say, can you see, can you feel, too?"

It cannot rationally be denied that LSD is sometimes dangerous. But schooling, too, justifies seriously weakening certain crucial human faculties in the young, in the interests of strengthening others, and drives some young people to suicide; nor does our society shield youth from the physical or moral dangers involved in defending it or extending its hegemony. Public concern over drug use is not aroused by real dangers, though there are some, but by the fact that pot and LSD are genuinely subversive of socialization. The madness, if madness it is, that the drugs induce is the direct converse of the kind of impairment that Erich Fromm calls a "socially patterned defect," that is, a distortion of character that society induces and rewards as adaptive to its institutions, though it be a far more permanent deformity in our capacity for human response than LSD induces in people who "drop acid." "Drop acid, not Napalm" seems a very suitable slogan for a psychedelic button.

The use of LSD and marijuana, in short, intensifies the eternal conflict, as ancient as the legend of Philoctetes, between those individuals whose sense of personal security is derived chiefly from reliance on order and control and is perpetually threatened by feeling, impulse, and human massiness and those who feel safest when they are in closest touch with their feelings but are perpetually threatened by repression and constraint. This conflict bears most heavily on the young, who not only are most exposed to and permitted fewer defenses against socializing forces but also are especially subject to the least liberal elements in society. School personnel and probation officers are selectively recruited from the respectable and relatively "up-tight" working and lower-middle classes. As I have suggested elsewhere, this is not merely an unfortunate accident but an essential social dynamic in a mass society determined to avoid the unrest that would continually arise if the most competent and perceptive youth were not taught thoroughly and, if need be, harshly to subordinate their sense of personal authority to the demands of the petit bourgeois. Hippie youth are harassed in virtually all schools, and the possibility of drug use brings the police, with their much greater commitment to order over impulsiveness, onto the scene.

If the police, when they arrived, acted merely to enforce the law when there was probable cause to believe that it was being broken, their action would be useful. But, particularly vis-à-vis hippie youth, the police act rather as the enforcers of a moral code that youth finds oppressive. Drug use by hippie youth provides the police with an otherwise comparatively rare opportunity to direct intense hostility against a member of a superordinate social class for an offense that the community holds to be vicious. The treatment of homosexuals is another example of this. Such occasions usually expose the victim to intense hatred as well as prosecution by the law. Conservative parents support the punitive authorities, while liberal parents are usually not much more sympathetic. Though the latter may not be so punitive, their liberalism inhibits them from defending their son or daughter very effectively against lower-status aggression, while a little elitism might have freed them to hire a good lawyer and publicly affirm family solidarity.

FOLK-ROCK MUSIC OF YOUTH

Still, the times are changing for adults as well as for youth. There are signs that our generation is becoming more open and expressive in its own behavior and attitudes. I refer to new forms of sensitivity training like T-groups, a growing willingness and even desire among college faculties to listen to students, which splits many faculties into hostile factions, one progressive and the other still "up-tight," and, particularly, the new respectful attention being given to the music of the young. The CBS-TV documentary on folk-rock featuring Leonard Bernstein, which appeared in the spring of 1967, was a genuine landmark. The music itself is quite extraordinary. Much of it is commercial kitsch, but what is extraordinary for our culture is that the most popular groups are rarely included among those with most prestige; the folk-rock subculture is, to that degree at least, aristocratic. The weekly list of the top 30 tunes rarely includes more than one or two records by the groups that are most respected and have the most to communicate to their audience.

Any adult who wants to receive a relatively complete message across the generation gap must learn to listen to this music and will probably derive great joy from it, as well as a strong mixture of less happy but equally appropriate emotions. No other art that is being produced in America or England currently has as much vitality or as much unity, in the sense that words and music are so well suited to each other and to what is jointly being expressed. It is characteristic of good folk-rock that the compositions really do not stand by themselves. If played and sung by someone other than the group who composed them, they become something different, usually poorer, though this music expands to become more like that for commercial hit tunes. If you dig the music, you will dig the youngsters, and, for this reason, it seems appropriate to provide the prospective listener with some specific guidance. Any such effort will, of course, be dated by the time it can be published, though more with respect to particular works than to groups; new ones may be omitted who have appeared too late to be included, but quality lasts.

It would be convenient to quote lyrics; but, on the whole, it would also be subtly misleading. Folk-rock devotees tend to be McLuhanites and would feel that the text separated from the music must necessarily give a false impression of the whole. This is true; one may quote lyrics to convey a specific idea from the music, but not of it. Even Bob Dylan, a major poet who certainly gives a reader more than most poets since Blake, gives a listener not only something more, but something different.

I have decided, therefore, instead to discuss briefly the major works of certain individuals and groups who, at the time of writing, seemed to have most to offer a new, but exacting, listener. These will be grouped according to functions.

High Art

Bob Dylan

The album *Bringing It All Back Home* (Columbia, CS2328) would be my choice for depth and range. These are not songs of social protest; they might be called songs that protest the human condition. In this album "The Gates of Eden" is most profound, and "Mr. Tambourine Man" and the more violently emotional "It's All Over Now, Baby Blue" are the most moving;

the shorter songs are among his most effective cosmic work, equally penetrating in their way.

Dylan, incidentally is, so far as I know, the only artist appealing primarily to the young whose work has been published in a special, expurgated version for adults. There exists an album called *The Metropolitan Pops Orchestra Plays Instrumental Versions of Bob Dylan Favorites* (Metro MS-597), the jacket of which notes, among other equally revealing comments, "You see, Bob Dylan is a brilliant, penetrating, indeed, shocking protest poet. So much so that the elder generations are often put off by his words (and his wild free-swing arrangements thereof). As a result, they miss some of the fabulous melodies underlying them. This 'Song Book' is designed to remedy that unfortunate circumstance most handsomely."

The Beatles

Since the Beatles have by now evolved to a point in their own development comparable to that achieved by Beethoven in the last quartets, they require more attention than the listener is sometimes able to give them after a long day's night. But the rewards are commensurate. Two of their latest albums, *Revolver* (Capitol ST 2576) and *Sgt. Pepper's Lonely Hearts Club Band* (Capitol SMAS-2653), are the best, though not the most immediately appealing. On *Revolver*, "Eleanor Rigby" and "Tomorrow Never Knows" are the most interesting musically, while "Yellow Submarine" is the most familiar. *Sgt. Pepper* is something more, a real song cycle or cantata, whose parts are so intricately related that they should not be appraised separately. It is light, compassionate, though completely unsentimental music; and older listeners will probably be struck first by the portions entitled "She's Leaving Home" and "When I'm Sixty-four," though the conclusion, "A Day in the Life," is all that a conclusion should be.

As a pleasant and musically worthwhile oddity, *The Baroque Beatles Book* (Elektra, BDS-7306) is a charmingly conceived fantasia based on early Beatle tunes by the Baroque Ensemble of the Merseyside Kammermusikgesellschaft, done with taste and wit.

Simon and Garfunkel

If Dylan is comparable to Blake, Paul Simon, who writes these songs, is comparable to Donne in his lighter work, though the idiom is wholly contemporary. Simon and Garfunkel will probably appeal more immediately to listeners accustomed to standard music than any other folk-rock artists; the delicacy and grace of their work takes them a long way from the Mothers or the Stones. Yet the underlying vision of society is not very different and is, at times, equally macabre. The best albums are *Sounds of Silence* (Columbia, CS 9269), with the heart-stopping song, "A Most Peculiar Man," and the later, more cheerful and controlled *Parsley, Sage, Rosemary and Thyme* (Columbia CS 9363), which includes the familiar "59th St. Bridge Song" properly sung, the lovely "Cloudy," and the intricate "The Dangling Conversation."

Donovan

The young Scotsman, Donavan Leitch, is one of the most enigmatic rock singers. I find his more recent work unpleasantly mannered and campy, but an earlier album, *Fairytale* (Hickory LPM 126), is the most beautiful record in my entire collection. One song on it, "The Ballad of the Crystal Man," is the most moving song I have ever heard. "Circus of Sour" is an utterly beguiling song, and "Sonny Goodge Street," which is being commercialized, should be heard here in its original form.

The Jefferson Airplane

This is probably the archetypical San Francisco rock group, though there are many listeners who would claim equal honor for The Grateful Dead — a very disciplined, intricate group, but a little too much like Bach mixed with napalm for my taste — The Quicksilver Messenger Service, or Big Brother and the Holding Company. The Airplane, however, seems to me to have a slight edge; it is more melodious without being any less exciting. *Surrealistic Pillow* (RCA LSP-3766) is their most representative album so far, with "Somebody to Love," the familiar "White Rabbit," "Plastic Fantastic Lover," and the lovely wordless little "Embryonic Journey" to remind us how much Scarlatti would have liked this music.

Low Art

The Mothers of Invention

Totally incomparable, this group is perhaps the most sophisticated of any rock group musically. They claim to be, and manifestly are, influenced by a variety of specific composers from Stravinsky to Stockhausen. Their idiom is so harsh that many listeners are turned off by it at once, but the work is perfect. Their second and latest album, *Absolutely Free* (Verve V/V605013), is, like *Sgt. Pepper*, a song cycle that cannot fairly be resolved into separate parts, though the Mothers themselves subtitle side 2 "The M.O.I. American Pageant" and refer to it as "32 in A Series of Underground Oratorios." This seems as good a name for it as any, from the opening "America Drinks" to the closing "America Drinks and Goes Home." If the album doesn't freak out the older listener — a risk the Mothers, who called their first album *Freakout*, joyfully assume — it will teach him more about dissenting youth than he probably really wants to know.

The Rolling Stones

By comparison with the elegance and fastidiousness of the Beatles' music, the Stones seem vulgar and obvious, but in their best work, they are artists of comparable quality. Actually, for people who do not dig rock, they are easier to comprehend than are the Beatles — which is also why listeners are easily offended by them. They draw on the whole British music hall tradition, and their best songs might be music hall songs: there is plenty of aggression in traditional Christmas pantomime, which is very similar to their work. There are many Stones' albums, but I prefer *Between the Buttons* (London PS 499). On this the song "Cool, Calm, Collected" is of special interest to the American listener; its subject is identified in the first verse as a very wealthy girl who is "dressed all in red, white and blue," and a brief musical quotation from "The Star-Spangled Banner" is used amusingly. The concluding song on the album, "Something Happened to Me Yesterday," is the most comical song I know. The Stones manage to make sheer, vitriolic hostility a beautiful emotion.

Two other newer British groups whom many listeners like, but whose integrity I am not yet sure of, are Fresh Cream and The Who. It costs very little to try them out.

The 13th Floor Elevators

Few rock critics will perhaps accept my rating this odd group so high, but it plays beautifully and with great originality. It is based in Houston, which is an interesting oddity in itself. The style is very far-out but melodious; one of the best songs on the album (International Artist 1 A — title same as the group), "I've Seen Your Face Before — (Splash 1)," makes use of what is essentially Gregorian chant. "Reverberation" is also a good and unusual song.

Occasional Pieces

There are many other groups whose work is of variable quality but who are good at their best and are, in any case, of special interest because they have produced single songs that particularly clearly express feelings or ideas that recur centrally in hippie dissent. Teeny-bopper resentment of pressures on them and of their lack of rights is very well expressed in The Seeds' hit song "You're Pushin' Too Hard" and in the Blues Magoos' "We Ain't Got Nothin' Yet." Both are forceful, rhythmic songs, of no particular musical distinction but very expressive. In the same vein, but subtler and much better musically, is Janis Ian's popular "Society's Child."

A very variable Los Angeles group, The Rainy Date, has created a song, written in rollicking parody of plastic Hawaiian-type music, about an elderly couple who go south singing "Hey-diddle-diddle, twenty-three, skiddool" in quest of "That Acapulco Gold," the title of the song and of the highest grade of marijuana. In utter contrast is a deeply moving, though rather mannered, song by the Daze called "And in My Mind Lives a Forest," which expresses the development of adolescent schizophrenia quietly and in clinically flawless imagery.

But the most interesting song of specific social comment is surely The Buffalo Springfield's "For What It's Worth," better known from its chorus as "Stop! Hey, What's That Sound?" This is an epic poem that recounts the incidents of the police battle on Sunset Strip last autumn, a haunting song in low key that first made me aware of the depth of meaning that folk-rock could convey.

Few adults seem to know this song, yet I have seen stacks of it in record stores all over the country and have heard it broadcast by local DJ's on small rock stations in central Georgia, where few of the youngsters who listened to it could have known precisely to what it referred. What they did know was that they had often felt the same way about other events in their own lives. Even in rural Georgia there is heat, and young people speaking their mind are receiving much resistance. The Springfield, as a group, really deserves more attention, but this one song so stands out in their total work that they themselves have adopted it as a kind of theme. Technically they are nearly as good as the Airplane, but they do not yet seem quite as certain what they are about. Unity may come.

This discussion could go on endlessly, but a listener who works his way into folk-rock with these guidelines will be able to find his own way thereafter, if he does not blow his mind. I have defined rock very narrowly, excluding race music and the excellent blues bands like Paul Butterfield's and Steve Miller's, which are becoming very popular with hippie youth. But they are not the work of youth and do not express the experience of youth. For not quite the same reason, I have excluded the work of The Mamas and the Papas, whom I very much admire and who are certainly not very old but seem so much more like guardian spirits of rock than like a rock group themselves. Their gifted comedienne, Cass, moreover, needs music no more than Bea Lillie does to do her thing, though she is a better and far more winning singer. The Mamas and the Papas are great but a listener would not learn much from their excellent performances about how young people feel.

The purpose of this musical critique has not been primarily to form the musical tastes of readers but to put them in touch with a group of works of art created by young people who are consummately aware of themselves and of what is happening to them in society. These artists speak of the patterns of generational conflict in which young people are so involved.

Systematic and Effective Innovation

Overviews

A PRACTICAL PLAN FOR
EDUCATIONAL REVOLUTION

Carl R. Rogers

Changingness must become the central element and aim of American education. Changingness can be defined as a process that is continuing, fluid, and adaptive — a continuing constructive turmoil. Such a process cannot be imposed on schools or their members; it must be self-directed and self-chosen, whether for the individual, the group, the organization, or the body politic.

The basic-encounter group or intensive group experience is an effective instrument for such self-directed change. It is a means of freeing an educational system to become involved in a continuing process of alteration and revitalization of the system and of the persons who make up the system.

This basic-encounter group must be relatively unstructured to provide a climate of maximum freedom for personal expression, exploration of feelings, and interpersonal communication. Such a climate of openness generates trust, which enables each person to recognize and change self-defeating attitudes, test and adopt innovative and constructive behaviors, and relate more effectively to others in his everyday life situation.

These encounters, then, contain the yeast of a revolution in the educational climate, a revolution that would bring about confidence in the process of learning and the process of change, rather than in the static transmission of knowledge that is stifling American education.

THE PROCESS OF EDUCATIONAL INNOVATION

Egon G. Guba

True educational improvement depends on the successful implementation of the four major phases of the change process: research, which provides one basis for invention; development, where practical solutions to existing problems are formulated; diffusion, where inventions are made available and understandable to the practitioner; and adoption, where inventions are adapted to local situations and implemented there.

The present implementation of each of these steps is hampered by certain problems, including overlapping and lack of communication in the process of change. One possible solution to these problems is a formulation in which responsibility for the change stages would be firmly fixed, each phase being designated to a specific educational organization.

INSTALLING AN INNOVATION

Louis J. Rubin

Using innovative paint to make a blue program red is not the solution to any educational problem. Educational innovation and improvement are related, but they certainly are not the same. Though schools must make a rational effort to capitalize on the new, they also should make an equal effort to correct old methods, even if the correctives prescribed may be five or ten years old.

To innovate, the four basic phases of the change process must be considered: research, development, dissemination, and installation. The installation phase is the most problematic and the most crucial to schools. To effectively install an innovation, educators first must make a preliminary analysis and then select an appropriate strategy. The difficulties at the core of a school or system must be examined, and adequate preparation must be made, including provisions for the retraining of personnel.

A Practical Plan for Educational Revolution

Carl R. Rogers

"EDUCATIONAL REVOLUTION" is a phrase that has been bandied about in recent years, a phrase connoting different ideas to different people. That revolution or change in education is desirable and necessary is agreed by all. In fact, it is terribly urgent that *changingness* become the central element and aim of American education. But the methods for carrying out this change are a matter of great debate and controversy.

The plan I am advocating necessitates an approach that views change not merely as a step going from a static here to a static there but as a continuing process that is fluid, adaptive, and, in effect, a continuing constructive turmoil. Furthermore, change must be self-directed, self-chosen change, whether for the individual, the group, the organization, or the body politic; change must not be imposed on schools or their members. An effective instrument for this self-directed change in persons, in groups, and in organizations does exist. This instrument is the intensive group experience, often called the basic-encounter group, the T-group, or the sensitivity-training group. This basic-encounter group is a significant means of freeing an educational system so that it can become involved in a self-directed changingness — a continuing process of alteration and revitalization of the organization and the persons who make up that organization.

CHANGINGNESS

The world itself is changing at an exponential rate. If our society is to meet the challenge of the dizzying changes in science, technology, communications, and social relationships, we cannot rely on the answers provided by the past but must put our trust in the processes by which new problems are met. For so quickly does change overtake us, that answers, knowledge, methods, and skills become obsolete almost at the moment of their achievement.

This constant flux implies that not only are new techniques needed for education but indeed a new goal is needed. In today's world, the goal of education must be to develop individuals who are open to change, who are flexible and adaptive, who have learned how to learn, and thus are able to learn continuously. Only such persons can meet constructively the perplexities of a world in which problems are spawned much faster than solutions. The goal of education must be to develop a society in which people can live comfortably with change rather than with rigidity. In the coming world, the capacity to face the new appropriately is more important than the ability to know and repeat the old.

Such a goal implies, in turn, that educators themselves must be open and flexible; they must be involved effectively in the processes of change. They must converse and convey the essential knowledge and values of the past; at the same time, they must welcome eagerly the innovations necessary to prepare for the unknown future.

A way must be found to develop, within the educational system as a whole as well as in each component, a climate conducive to personal growth — a climate in which innovation is not frightening and in which the creative capacities of administrators, teachers, and students are nourished and expressed rather than stifled. A way must be found to develop a climate in which the focus is not upon teaching but on the facilitating self-directed learning. Only then can we develop the creative individual, the individual who is open to all of his experience, aware of it, and accepting it, and thus is continually in the process of changing. Only in this way can we bring about the creative educational organization that also will be continually in the process of changing.

Forty years of working with troubled individuals have convinced me that nearly all individuals have within themselves the capacity to move and grow in a socialized and self-fulfilling direction, provided that they can be exposed to a growth-promoting personal climate — a relationship of realness, of caring, of empathy. The same is true of groups and organizations. There are those who, out of a sense of urgency, wish to impose change because they regard growth as too slow, but this desire negates the basic principles of our democracy. We must instead try to promote growth.

Intensive Group Experience

One of the most effective means yet discovered for facilitating growth, change, and constructive learning — in individuals or in the organizations they compose — is the intensive group experience. This intensive group or workshop or encounter group usually consists of ten to fifteen persons and a facilitator or leader. It is relatively unstructured and provides a climate of maximum freedom for personal expression, exploration of feelings, and interpersonal communication. Emphasis is upon the interactions among the group members in an atmosphere that encourages each to drop his defenses and façades. Thus, individuals are enabled to relate directly and openly to other members of the group in a basic encounter. Individuals then come to know themselves and each other more fully than is possible in the usual social or working relationships; the climate of openness, risk-taking, and honesty generates trust, permitting them to recognize and change self-defeating attitudes, test and adopt more innovative and constructive behaviors, and, subsequently, relate more adequately and effectively to others in their everyday life situations.

Since the mid-1940's, such workshops have been used extensively by groups considered to be normal and well-functioning — corporation presidents, industrial executives, government administrators, professional groups, and laymen — under a wide variety of auspices, of which the National Training Laboratory is perhaps the best known (Benne, Bradford, and Lippitt, 1964).

Generally the aim of these intensive group experiences is to improve the learning and abilities of the participants in such areas as leadership and interpersonal communication. Another aim is to bring about change in the organizational climates and structures in which the members work. Characteristically, these group experiences are conducted as an intensive residential experience in which the participants live and meet together for periods ranging from three days to two or three weeks.

Educational Group Experience

Within the past several years, educators have begun to make use of the intensive group experience to a small extent. In the educational setting, the aims have been to release the participants' capacity for better educational leadership through improved interpersonal relationships or to foster learning by the whole person. The results of such group experiences have been promising. Still, there has been almost no attempt to utilize the intensive group experience in a coherent approach to change in a total public educational system. Hence, all too commonly, a teacher or faculty member returns from such an experience ready to behave in new and changing ways, only to discover that his attitudes are not welcomed in a "stable and well-regulated" educational organization. Two alternatives are open: (1) he returns reluctantly to his previous conventional behavior or (2) he becomes a puzzling and disruptive influence, neither understood nor approved in his institution.

It seems quite clear that this new tool for change cannot be used in the most effective manner unless the whole system is moving toward changingness, accommodating change in its own personnel and in its own units. Industry is already learning this. This principle of opening up the possibilities for change in the whole system during a relatively short period of time is the essence of my dream.

Hypotheses of the Intensive Group Experience

In the whole area of intensive group experience, practice has far outrun theory and research, largely because of lack of university, foundation, and governmental support. Consequently these hypotheses have often been validated in practice but only modestly supported by research:

1. A group facilitator can help to develop a psychological climate of safety in which freedom of expression and reduction of defensiveness gradually occur.

2. In such a psychological climate, many of the immediate feelings of each member toward others and toward himself tend to be expressed.

3. A climate of mutual trust develops out of this freedom to express real feelings, positive and negative. Each member moves toward greater acceptance of his total being — his emotional, intellectual, and physical being as it is, with its potential.

4. With individuals less inhibited by defensive rigidity, the possibility of change — in personal attitudes and behavior, in teaching methods, in administrative methods — becomes less threatening.

5. With a reduction of defensive rigidity, individuals can hear

each other and learn from each other to a greater extent.

6. There is a development of feedback from one person to another, in which each individual learns how he appears to others and what impact he has in interpersonal relationships.

7. As individuals hear each other more accurately, an organization tends to become a relationship of persons with common goals rather than a formal hierarchical structure.

8. With this greater freedom and improved communication, new ideas, new concepts, and new directions emerge. Innovation becomes a desirable rather than a threatening possibility.

9. These learnings in the group experience tend to carry over, temporarily or permanently, into the relationships with peers, students, subordinates, and superiors following the group experience.

A PLAN FOR EDUCATIONAL CHANGE

Having described the need for educational change and the intensive group experience as the tool or process by which it might be brought about, I would like now to present a specific plan for implementation. Every element of this plan has been tried and found to be effective either in industry, in education, or with other groups. Experienced personnel are available throughout the country who have the attitudes and know-how to carry out these activities. It is the weaving of these elements into a comprehensive plan that constitutes its novelty.

Such a plan could be applied to any educational organization or to a number of them simultaneously. The plan would be equally effective in an elementary school system, an elementary–secondary system, a junior college, a college or university, or a graduate school. One might find some increase in the degree of rigidity as one progresses to a higher level, but the same principles would apply, with some common-sense modification of specifics to meet each situation.

Selection of Target System

The only criterion for selecting a target system for changingness is that one or more individuals in power be desirous of change and be willing to involve themselves in a basic-encounter group. If they are willing to experience the changes that come about in such a group, they can then make reasonable judgments about the next steps that should be undertaken.

From among several possibilities, a target system has been selected that meets this criterion. The system is composed of Immaculate Heart College in Los Angeles, a teacher-training institution, and the 60 parochial elementary and high schools in the Los Angeles and San Diego dioceses that it staffs or supervises — approximately 10 high and 50 elementary schools. Other reasons prompted the choice of Immaculate Heart College for this experiment. For one thing, the situation provided an opportunity to affect teacher training as well as the structure and personnel of individual schools. For another, this constituted a highly challenging situation since parochial schools are regarded as, and often are, inferior to public schools, and the fact that many of the teachers trained by Immaculate Heart College go into the Los Angeles public school system suggested possible wider ramifications in the future.

An Encounter Group for Administrators and Faculty

Thus far, after one joint planning session, one step of the program has been detailed, and the other steps have been projected in a rough outline.

The first step will be an encounter group experience for all who volunteer from the administration and faculty of the college. This group encounter will be held in an off-campus conference center. Since it would be difficult to get such a group together for a solid week, these 80 people will meet for two weekends, spaced a month or two apart. The workshop will have some general sessions, but the largest amount of time will be spent in seven or eight basic-encounter groups. The facilitators for these groups will be supplied from the pool of experienced individuals who have worked in such a capacity for Western Behavioral Sciences Institute.

These groups will be relatively unstructured, and if past experience is any guide, exploration of current interpersonal feelings and relationships will become a major focus. Often gripes and feuds, which for years have prevented real communication, come to the surface and are resolved in the eight or ten hours per day of intensive group meetings. Too, this type of group provides the administrator with a microcosm for studying the problems he faces, and the problems he creates, in his own organization. Through confrontation, he discovers how he appears to others. He also has the opportunity to experiment with and try out new modes of behavior in a relatively safe situation.

What will happen in two such intensive weekends? It is almost impossible to convey the quality of the relationships that develop. From my past experiences, certain people and feelings immediately come to mind:

Administrators who have worked together for 20 years discover they have never known each other at all as persons. . . . Negative feelings, which have hurt planning and work for years, now can safely be brought into the open, understood, and dissolved as can positive feelings that have always seemed too risky to voice. . . . Ideals and hopes, which have seemed too fantastic to share with others. . . . Quick angers, which strengthen rather than destroy relationships because they are expressed in a context of trust and openness. . . . Personal tragedies and problems, the expression of which make penetrable barriers behind which some individuals have hidden and from behind which they begin to emerge. . . . An intense sense of community, which develops in place of the alienation and personal loneliness each has felt. . . . The willingness to risk new behaviors, new directions, and new purposes. . . . The determination to rebuild family relationships as well as organizational procedures.

These are only a few of the manifestations that occur in an intensive group experience in which individuals, who have interacted only in their functional roles as president, dean, board member, professor, or supervisor, begin to interact as persons.

What may we expect as outcomes of such an experience for the trustees, presidents, deans, faculty, principals, supervisors, or administrative specialists in various fields? What might we expect in your own administrative group? Some of the probable outcomes are described in the following statements:

The Administrator

1. Will be less protective of his own constructs and beliefs and hence be more capable of listening accurately to other administrators and to faculty members;

2. Will find it easier and less threatening to accept innovative ideas;

3. Will have less need for the protection of bureaucratic rules and, therefore, will decide issues more on the basis of merit;

4. Will communicate more clearly to superiors, peers, and subordinates because his communications will be oriented more toward an openly declared purpose and less toward covert self-protection;

5. Will be more person-oriented and thus more democratic in staff or faculty meetings;

6. Will draw more widely and deeply on the resource potential of his faculty and staff;

7. Will be more likely to face and openly confront personal emotional frictions, which develop between himself and his colleagues, rather than bury the conflict under new "regulations" or avoid it in other ways;

8. Will be more able to accept feedback from his staff, both positive and negative, and to use it as constructive insight into himself and his behavior;

9. Will be more able to communicate realistically with his board of trustees and thus possibly lay the groundwork for altering the organizational structure of the educational system.

Subsequent Encounter Groups

Other workshops or encounter groups that will follow this initial group experience for administrators will be similar in process and context. About 80 persons will be involved in each of the subsequent workshops, which will include the following people: teachers-in-training at the college and the faculty members who teach them; the administrators of the parochial schools — principals, vice-principals, deans, and supervisors; teachers in these schools; parents; and students, teachers, and administrators in classroom units, both at the elementary and high school level. In the last group, students and teachers will have the opportunity to communicate as persons rather than as roles to learn something of the feelings that exist on both sides in the classroom.

The most exciting kind of group — the one that slices vertically through the whole system — constitutes the next step in the program. If it were a public school, there would be present in this group, on a voluntary basis, some members of the board of education, at least two parents, a superintendent, a principal, teachers, a few bright students, and some failing students or school dropouts. Since such a group might have difficulty getting under way, it could be brought together under some such theme as "Our School: What I Like and Don't Like About It and What I Want It to Be."

The person who has never been involved in a group experience may believe it impossible for such a diverse group of individuals truly to communicate. Yet very similar groups have been conducted, with extremely rewarding results. When a board member reaches the point where he can hear the hatred and contempt of the dropout for the schools and the reasons for those negative feelings, when the teacher discovers that the board member is not merely a figure of authority but a human being, often with mixed and insecure feelings about the role he is attempting to play, when the "A" student learns that others less brilliant are sometimes more perceptive in the realm of feeling than he, when a parent finds he can truly learn from an adolescent and vice-versa, when widely divergent criticisms of and hopes for the schools are brought fully into the open, examined, and challenged in the context of emotion in which they exist, and when mutual trust grows in a climate that includes mutual differences, then we can say with considerable assurance that no person in the group will remain unchanged. Each will have achieved a broader understanding of self and others. Each will, to some degree, have become more flexible. Each will find that he is involved in changingness.

Even a very few such vertical groups would drastically change the climate and the flavor of any educational system. Though it has been described in terms most appropriate to a secondary school, it can be utilized at any level. At any level it contains the yeast of a revolution in the educational climate.

The Time Table

In carrying out the plan as outlined thus far, it is essential that the various group experiences should be held within a reasonably short period of time, so that the impact will not be dissipated. Our aim will be to hold six to nine workshops during the first academic year of the program, with seven or eight encounter groups in each of these workshops. There would also be the opportunity for follow-up group sessions for groups whose members felt that some serious problems were left unresolved. Thus, at a minimum, the number of people involved in the intensive group experience will run into the hundreds, this being a sufficient fraction of the total administrative, faculty, and student body so that the effects will not be lost but will serve as a continuing ferment.

Plan for Continuing Change

Concurrently with these group encounters, a capability for continuing change must be built into the system so that a larger and larger fraction of its members may also have the opportunity for one or more intensive group experiences. It is important that the initial staff of outside facilitators be able to withdraw, retaining only a consultant function, if that is desired.

Training Facilitators

To facilitate the withdrawal of the outside staff and to afford a large proportion of people the chance to participate, those who have participated in the preceding workshops will be given opportunity to apply for further training as group facilitators. From these applicants, a number will be selected, not so much on the basis of academic background but on the basis of attitudes. The person who is relatively nondefensive, who relates in a genuine way to others, who is aware of and can express his feelings, who is capable of empathy with the feelings of others, and who has shown that he cares for others in a nonpossessive way will be the type of person selected.

Such individuals will be given further experience in residential training workshops in which there will be ample opportunity for reading, listening to recordings of groups, and seeing movies of group experience and interpersonal relationships.

After such preparation, each trainee can work as a cofacilitator with a member of the outside staff in conducting groups during the ensuing year. When it is mutually agreed that he is competent to handle groups on his own, he will do so, with one or more outside staff members serving as consultants.

In this way, a foundation will be laid for an ongoing change and ferment in the system. Further group experiences for faculty members, parents, and administrators can take place. New vertical groups can be formed. By this time too, new ways of working, impossible now to foresee, will have been developed and can be tried out. Thus, as the original professional group withdraws to a less active role, the educational system will have incorporated into itself a facilitative function that will mean continuous openness to innovation, continuous change.

RISKS AND OBJECTIONS

Thus far the plan has been presented in positive terms. What are its dangers? What criticisms may be made of it? In what ways may it go wrong?

Possible Damage to Individuals

There is often fear that the openness of a group experience and the revealing of heretofore hidden feelings may result in damage to the person. This risk exists, but it is very small. In follow-up questionnaires of nearly 500 persons who had been members of groups for which I had been responsible, only two felt that the experience had been damaging rather than helpful. This is a serious matter and one that needs further study, but the minuteness of the percentage affected badly indicates that the fear of psychological damage to persons involved is almost entirely unjustified.

Possibility of Too Rapid Change

Administrators, particularly those who have prided themselves on the efficiency of their organization, may fear that the plan as outlined would produce too much change. It cannot be denied that when problems, especially interpersonal problems, are faced openly rather than being hidden, when interpersonal relationships are substituted in place of roles and rules, and when learning and its facilitation rather than teaching becomes the focus of education, a certain amount of constructive turbulence is inevitable. It should be stressed that the proposed plan does not pretend to solve all problems; instead it substitutes the problems of a process-centered organization for those of an organization aimed toward static stability.

Possible Rejection by Community

The plan outlined would set the educational system on a path or a direction rather sharply different from that of the ordinary school system. This involves the risk of too great a discrepancy between the directions approved by the community and the directions being taken. This risk has been partially decreased by the involvement of board members and parents in the intensive group experience. Yet, it cannot be denied that in every community there are individuals and groups who are devoted to a return to the past, who hold rigid views of what a school or university should be, and who are deeply frightened by freedom of thought, choice, action, and by the rapid changes characterizing the modern world. Since these individuals and groups would be unlikely to avail themselves of opportunities for an intensive group experience precisely because it might involve change, they represent a difficult problem to which no easy or pat answer seems possible.

Possible Criticism by Professional Groups

One element of the plan that is likely to arouse criticism and even indignation on the part of psychologists, psychiatrists, and others professionally involved in the field of interpersonal relationships is the training of faculty members and administrators as group facilitators. The argument is that full professional training with a Ph.D. or an M.D. is essential if an individual is to undertake such a function. But there is solid evidence that this is a mistaken view. An outstanding example of this evidence is the work of Rioch (1963), which proved that selected housewives can be given training in a year's time that enables them to carry on therapy with disturbed individuals — therapy that in its quality is indistinguishable from the work of experienced professionals. Thus, the goal and procedure outlined has good precedent; however, this does not guarantee that it will be free from attack by professional groups.

RESEARCH

The plan also involves research; for example, a general assessment will be made of the change or lack of change in the schools that have been involved. This assessment will be prepared by experienced educators who are skilled in making appraisals of educational systems — the quality of learning achieved, the receptiveness to innovations, and the levels of organizational morale. There will also be rigorous before-and-after measurement of changes in the attitudes and behavior of individuals in a sampling of the groups. Finally the organizational climate and structure in a sampling of the schools will be measured before and after the initiation of the program.

The procedure I have presented is appropriate to the educational needs of our present culture. It is a plan capable of being reproduced in many educational systems at all levels, a plan that can be carried on, if not inaugurated, by catalysts within the system itself, and it is a program that draws on the natural, built-in motivation for growth and change that exists in every individual and is latent in every organization. Furthermore, it is a program that does not depend on a submissive acceptance of changes suggested from the outside; and most importantly, this is a plan for educational change that could result in the kind of educational revolution needed — a revolution that would bring about confidence in the process of learning and the process of change, rather than in the static transmission of knowledge that is stultifying American education and the very future of America, which depends, after all, on her citizens and their capability for changingness as a way of life.

The Process of Educational Improvement

Egon G. Guba

INNOVATION IS today the exciting keyword in education. In a major effort to improve our schools, we are initiating change all across the nation. To be effective in such innovation, however, we must first be knowledgeable about the very process of change, and we must improve upon the existing execution of the steps of this process.

A MODEL OF THE CHANGE PROCESS

Steps in the Change Process

What constitutes the process of change? The change process may be viewed as consisting of four major phases or steps: research, development, diffusion, and adoption. Each has different objectives and a different contribution to make to change.

Research

Research, for example, has as its basic objective the advancement of knowledge. The researcher is not to be concerned with practical applications of his ideas. He needs freedom to pursue his ideas wherever they lead, he needs to be free to fail on occasion, and he needs to be free from pressures for an immediate result.

Despite any apparent lack of connection between research and practice, research does have an important part to play in relation to change — it can provide one basis for invention. In formulating a program to deal with the reading difficulties of culturally disadvantaged children, for example, one could hardly ignore existing research on reading, cultural differences, motivation, and development.

Development

Development, the second step in the change process, has as its basic objective the identification of operating problems and the formulation of solutions to those problems. The developer constantly must probe the system to determine sources of difficulty and must then devise new approaches and techniques to ameliorate or eliminate whatever problems he may identify. In devising such solutions, the developer borrows heavily from various sources — from research, from experts, and from his own experience.

But development implies more than just supplying an answer. The answer must work in the real world, must be adaptable to the system, must be usable by available personnel, and must achieve effective results. Thus, development involves production, engineering, packaging, and testing a proposed problem, solution, or invention.

Diffusion

The most potent solutions that man can devise to overcome his problems have little utility if practitioners know little about them or have little opportunity to discover how the solutions work. The purpose of diffusion is to create awareness and provide opportunities for the assessment of the invention. Diffusion, in short, makes the invention available and understandable to the practitioner.

Adoption

Adapting an invention to the local situation and installing it are the purposes of adoption. Such activity presents many difficulties. Every situation has its own peculiarities; thus, an invention cannot simply be slipped into place without considerable modification to itself, to the system, or to both. A prudent local administrator should test the innovation before assimilating it as a component part of his system. This assimilation may involve training local personnel, arranging appropriate scheduling, modifying available space, and the like. The adoption process, therefore, establishes the invention as part of the ongoing program and, in time, converts it into a "non-innovation."

Activities Involved in Each Step of the Change Process

Having defined the steps in the change process, we must now consider the activities undertaken by the researcher, the developer, the diffuser, and the adopter in carrying out their missions.

Research

All possible research activities can be placed in four categories: *depicting, relating, conceptualizing,* and *testing.*

When a researcher approaches a new topical area about which little is known, there is little he can do other than generally describe or depict the phenomena of interest in qualitative or quantitative form.

After a sufficient amount of depiction takes place, it becomes possible for the researcher to relate depicted entities.

With a sufficiently developed network of relationships, the researcher can formulate questions that lead directly to conceptualization or attempts to account for the observed depictions and relations.

These efforts at explanation can then be tested further to determine the validity of the conceptualization. In this testing process, many of the same techniques used in the depicting and relating stages may be used again; typically, however, experimental methodology is employed to test the hypothesis in a controlled environment.

Development

Like research, development can be similarly categorized. Its four phases are *depicting, inventing, fabricating,* and *testing.*

The developer's first job is to depict the state of affairs so that problems can be identified. The developer must then invent solutions to the problems. Such invention may take a variety of forms: the application of an existing solution, the adoption of a direct analog, the conversion of an indirect analog, the combination of several alternative solutions, or the introduction of a completely new solution. These five different possible ways of arriving at a proposed solution of a problem can be termed *transmitting, translating, transforming, synthesizing,* and *creating.*

The fact that a solution is identified does not signify that it is ready for application. Materials have to be developed and combined into appropriate sequences; the technique to be applied must fit into other ongoing school activities. Such activities may be designated as fabrication, a term intended to cover the entire gamut of engineering and packaging phases that may be required to make the innovation "market ready."

Finally, the proposed solution must undergo a comprehensive trial to determine if refinements are necessary. Such a trial must take place in authentic school situations; otherwise, the applicability of the findings to the real world of education are dubious indeed.

Diffusion

The third step in the change process, diffusion, involves six basic techniques: *telling, showing, helping, involving, training,* and *intervening.*

Telling comprises communicating by the written or spoken word. A direct confrontation with the phenomena of interest, as in a planned or casual observation or in actual participation, can be termed showing.

Helping differs from telling or showing in that it necessitates direct involvement of the diffuser in the affairs of the adopter *on the adopter's terms.* It may take the form of consultation, service, trouble-shooting, and the like. One may also involve the adopter in diffusion by enlisting him to assist with the development, testing, or packaging of an innovation, to act as a "satellite" or agent to cause others to adopt, or to identify the problems to which innovative solutions are to be sought. Or the diffusion agent can train the adopter, familiarizing him with features of a proposed innovation or assisting him to increase his skills and competencies or to alter his attitudes.

Another diffusion technique is intervening, in which the diffusion agent is directly involved with the adopter, but *on the agent's terms.* This may take the form of mandating certain actions, inserting certain control mechanisms, or engineering certain economic or political factors.

Adoption

The adopter shapes and installs an innovation within a particular local setting. Adoption involves at least three major steps: *trial, installation,* and *institutionalization.*

Trial is certainly essential to adoption. No prudent administrator will permit the installation of an innovation on a permanent basis without having convinced himself that it will perform as claimed. Indeed, a local trial is mandatory even when national assessments have indicated that the innovation performs well on the average, for the obvious reason that the situation in which installation is proposed may not be average.

After the innovation is tested, it can then be installed. However, four factors must be given consideration in installing the innovation: modification, training, facilities, and administration. The adopter must determine whether alterations in the innovation itself or in the school situation are necessary. Personnel must then be trained to use the proposed innovation.

In installing the innovation, the adopter must also consider the physical needs such as arrangement and equipment. Finally, problems in scheduling, budgeting, staffing, organizing, and so on, must be studied.

Ultimately the innovation must be assimilated into the ongoing program. At some time it must cease to be viewed as an innovation and become an integral and accepted component. Although the steps necessary to insure institutionalization are unclear, the most important factor may be simply the passage of time. Obviously the lack of awkward incidents in relation to the innovation is helpful, and the more quickly the spotlight can be taken off the invention, the more quickly it is likely to become accepted.

EXISTING EFFORTS IN THE PROCESS OF CHANGE

If this model for change has validity, we should now determine who carries out each step. What mechanisms now exist or what mechanisms are needed to do the research, the development, the diffusion, and the adoption that the model calls for? How successful are existing approaches?

Research

The research enterprise in the United States has certain dimensions that are crucial in determining the kinds of research done, and by whom. These dimensions are: *loose organization, university base, individual direction, theory orientation, experimental commitment, psycho-statistical tradition, part-time nature,* and *federal funding.*

First, there is a wide variety of agencies and individuals that conduct educational research without any central organization or coordination. This arrangement has the obvious virtues of flexibility and simplicity but suffers from the fact that it is difficult to enlist the efforts of a number of persons or agencies in pursuit of a common research objective. Thus, communication becomes difficult, and resources cannot be allocated in an optimal manner.

Most educational research is conducted by university personnel rather than by persons employed by other agencies. The university has the professional manpower and an inexpensive labor pool in the form of graduate students, and the university's traditional posture makes possible the high-risk taking and sanctioned freedom to fail required by the researcher. However, the university's traditional interest in new and basic knowledge militates against the more practical research that the real world of education needs.

Topics for research are chosen predominantly on the basis of the interests of the individual investigator. Thus, researchers are free to pursue that which concerns them most deeply and to which they are most committed. But this posture militates against programmatic, team-research efforts that have so effectively dealt with practical problems in other fields such as medicine, nuclear energy, or space flight.

Moreover, much educational research is conducted by persons from related social and behavioral disciplines such as psychology and sociology. The research thus tends to relate to the theories of those disciplines rather than to the solution of educational problems. This approach obviously has good results for the related discipline, but meager results for the practice of education in general.

In most research, the experiment is considered to be the only proper format for scientific inquiry. Non-experimental approaches are seen as inferior or misleading. This is not surprising, since the experimental method has in fact achieved great breakthroughs in other areas of science and the methods and instruments of experimentalism are well explicated and available. On the other hand, it is apparent that the assumptions underlying the experimental method are not well met in the world of educational practice, and application of the method may often lead to trivial or misleading findings.

Educational research is conducted in the main by persons whose training is heavily based in educational psychology, statistics, and measurement theory. In general, such research is afforded a cohesiveness and focus that would be hard to achieve in other ways. On the other hand, this general agreement upon one tradition serves to exclude other possible tra-into the prevailing orientation.
ditions, causes, problem areas, and methods that do not fit

Educational research also suffers from its part-time nature, since it is usually conducted by persons who have other demanding duties, primarily teaching. Very few persons are able to devote as much as one-third of their time to research, making it difficult for the researcher to maintain conceptual continuity and sustained effort.

Finally, since most educational research is funded by the federal government, the ever-present specter of federal control has generally kept federal monies from being spent in a systematic and coordinated way. Communication has not been substantially improved by federal funding, nor have linkages between the research community and other parts of the educational establishment been well developed.

The existence of this particular pattern for conducting research thus has both good and bad consequences. There is no doubt that American educational research is in the vanguard in terms of scope, creativity, flexibility, rigor, excitement, and support, but in relation to educational practice, this form of organization also results in at least three problem areas.

First, it is clear that research is not utilized by practitioners. The practitioner often has difficulty in finding definitive and helpful data. No massive educational research effort has been undertaken; rather almost all research activity has taken the form of ad hoc project efforts. Further, research has been quite unresponsive to practical problems, perhaps because of the lack of appropriate input and output channels.

Second, mechanisms for linking research with the world of practice are almost nonexistent. New specializations have not been developed to meet some of these linking needs, perhaps because practice is generally viewed as a low-status activity by university-based researchers. Of course, such problems as a low supply of funds and lack of personnel have necessitated and dictated emphasis upon central rather than peripheral matters; thus, the research community clearly, and properly, regards the production of new knowledge as more central than the development of practical applications.

Third, programs for training additional researchers and/or new research specializations are also inadequate. Practicing researchers are being asked to perform functions for which they were not adequately trained, and the roles that are emerging pose entirely new training demands.

Thus, we must answer with some ambivalence the question of who is doing educational research and with what success. Obviously there is a large educational research establishment successfully engaging in the kinds of activities to which it has been traditionally committed, but the establishment is not influencing the world of practice to any great degree. Certainly, as my colleague Henry M. Brickell has suggested, "School practice in this nation cannot be understood as being based primarily upon research." For the foreseeable future, it seems likely that advancement at other stages of the change process will continue to be relatively independent of what happens at the research stage.

The federal government is making one effort to circumvent

this problem through the establishment of research and development centers. Although these centers have as yet shown little capability for shaking off the traditional constraints, particularly in terms of developing programmatic foci that can be studied systematically and in depth, it is undoubtedly too early to predict whether such developments will occur.

Development

Until a few years ago, it had not occurred to anyone in the educational establishment that development was a necessary function. Practitioners commonly assumed that development was properly the concern of the researchers, while the researchers felt that it was the practitioners who should derive applications from research.

The plain fact is, of course, that development is a very complicated process that neither practitioners nor researchers are particularly competent to carry out. Rather, high-level specialists are required to do the job. Moreover, development depends not only upon the availability of relevant basic research but also upon a host of other factors as well: the availability of resources, institutional support, experience, practical judgment, political factors, and the like. Research data provide only one of several critical inputs, and the blending of these inputs requires more specialized skill than either researchers or practitioners commonly possess.

In recent months, there have been some systematic attempts to establish development agencies. Clearly the research and development centers established under the Cooperative Research Act have a mandate to turn their research into practice. Yet successful development involves a great deal more than the mere availability of relevant research. Perhaps the primarily research-oriented research and development centers are not suited to the task. The recently established regional educational laboratories, under Title III of the Elementary and

Secondary Education Act, which are mandated to identify and solve educational problems, may prove successful development agencies. Thus far, however, they are too new to venture a judgment about their probable level of success.

It is apparent that no existing agencies have responsibility for the full range of development activities indicated by the change analysis. The depicting function seems to be especially neglected. While both regional laboratories and Title III projects were mandated to survey their regional needs, it is clear that these surveys were carried out in a most perfunctory way. Even when well done, these surveys could provide only a static "snapshot" of the situation at any moment rather than a dynamic "motion picture film" over an appreciable time span.

The invention function is perhaps better managed than the others. Funds are available for improvement projects, and several agencies, including the new industry-education combines as well as the regional laboratories and research and development centers, are beginning to undertake massive improvement projects. Yet we still know far too little about effective ways of creating new solutions or even of transmitting, translating, or transforming known solutions.

Fabrication — engineering and packaging — will probably be handled best by the industry-education combines since these typically involve publishers and manufacturers of hardware. The publishing industry has shown a great deal of ingenuity in the past in placing its materials into interesting and novel formats and will probably continue to do so.

Testing is another area of development that is quite underdeveloped. Existing evaluation designs seem inappropriate for the real problems of education, and commercial agencies are often overeager to rush their fabrications into production without the kinds of testing that would assure a professionally warrantable product. Thus, both conceptual and consumer-protection innovations are needed in the area of testing.

From one point of view then, the development picture is not good. However, since education is now fully aware of the need for development activities, is apprised of their complexity, and is being aided with resources to start development activity, perhaps most of those problems enumerated will have disappeared within a decade.

Diffusion

Diffusion is a step in the change process that is regarded with some distaste by many members of the educational establishment, particularly the research community. Traditionally educational diffusion has been the domain of commercial interests, mainly book publishers. Recently both research and development centers and regional educational laboratories were given some diffusion responsibilities, and these agencies have begun to develop new approaches.

The major diffusion responsibility, however, seems to be falling squarely on the shoulders of Title III projects. The Office of Education Manual for Project Applicants for Title III grants clearly defines as one of the primary objectives of the program "creating an awareness of new programs and services of high quality that can be incorporated in school programs." The manual also points out that "PACE seeks to . . . demonstrate worthwhile innovations in educational practice through exemplary programs."

Since diffusion seems to be such an important responsibility for Title III projects, I shall later return to this topic.

Adoption

Even less developed than diffusion on the change continuum is adoption. The traditional university-based field service bureau is perhaps the one existing agency that might be said to be concerned with this phase, but, such service bureaus have not been very successful for a variety of reasons. There were not enough of them to fulfill the need; they lacked the resources to do a thorough job; and they fell into repetitive and mediocre patterns of operation that rendered them essentially incapable of behaving resourcefully and innovatively.

One might argue that the adoption task might be appropriate for state departments of education, but these agencies are confronted not only with the same problems as the university field service bureaus but also with fear of government control. For this reason they do not hold much promise as adoption agencies.

Perhaps the adoption activity should be assigned to the local school. Each school district could develop adoption units to assist local personnel in accomplishing the necessary initiation, installation, and institutionalization. But not every school district is in a position to establish such an agency. For one thing there are probably too few personnel available to accomplish the necessary tasks. Moreover, the establishment of such a unit in every school district might constitute unnecessary proliferation.

It would appear then that there is at present no effective solution to the adoption problem. It is clear, however, that until this gap in the change process continuum is closed, we cannot expect school improvement to occur smoothly and effectively.

DIFFUSION AND TITLE III

The purpose of diffusion activities is to create awareness and understanding of an invention and to provide opportunities for its assessment. Such a purpose clearly requires that contact be made with the potential adopter and that the diffusion activity be shaped to fit him. Strategies must be developed that will cause the adopter to accept, or at least seriously consider, the proposed innovation. Such strategies are determined by the implicit or explicit assumptions made about the nature of the adopter.

Strategies

At least seven diffusion strategies are in current use, each of which depends upon a different formulation of the nature of the adopter. These are *value, rational, didactic, psychological, economic, political,* and *authority strategies.*

Using the value strategy, the adopter is viewed as a professionally oriented entity who can be obligated to adopt through an appeal to his values. Thus, for instance, appeals can be made on behalf of "what is best for the children." With the rational strategy, the adopter is viewed as a rational entity who can be convinced, on the basis of hard data and logical argument, of the utility, the feasibility, effectiveness, and efficiency of the innovation. Or one can use the didactic strategy in which the adopter is viewed as a willing, but untrained entity — one who has the appropriate values, motivations, and the necessary economic resources but does not know how to perform. He can, therefore, be taught what is needed to achieve adoption.

The adopter can also be viewed as a psychological entity whose needs for acceptance, involvement, and inclusion can be employed to persuade him to adopt. Viewing the adopter as an economic entity, the diffusion agent compensates him for agreeing to adopt or deprives him of resources for refusing to adopt. Finally, using the authority strategy, the adopter is viewed as an entity in a bureaucratic system who can be compelled to adopt by virtue of his relationships to an authority hierarchy.

Each of these strategies can then be related to the six diffusion techniques: telling, showing, helping, involving, training, and intervening. Thus what one would tell in relation to a rational strategy — scientific facts — is quite different from what one would tell in relation to a psychological strategy — shared experiences. The diffuser following the psychological strategy would design his "showing" less to illustrate solutions to problems than to uncover the enthusiasm of the participating teachers. His training would be concerned less with developing skills than in sensitizing the participants in the area of human relations. And so on.

Difficulties in Use of Strategies and Techniques

Why, given such an impressive array of strategies and techniques, do we not enjoy greater success in diffusing innovations? Certain difficulties hamper current diffusion efforts, including those of Title III projects.

For one thing, diffusion techniques are often mistaken for diffusion strategies. This confusion has three disastrous consequences. First, it causes the diffuser to focus on means rather than upon the image of the practitioner. Second, it results in the design of a badly integrated diffusion program; thus the particular techniques that are selected may make only a fortuitous contribution toward getting the adopter to adopt and may, in fact, be working at cross-purposes. Third, it may result in an erroneous utilization of techniques; thus the diffuser may fail to make the adaptations required for a particular audience because he does not have a clear image of that audience guiding his activities. So he may, for example, insist on filling his newsletters with evaluative information when he should be stressing value patterns.

Further, uni-dimensional strategies are being advocated to the exclusion of other strategies. It is likely that no single strategy is sufficient to accomplish adequate diffusion. Yet, in many instances, diffusion strategies are advocated that depend upon the assumption that one of these aspects greatly outweighs the others. For example, it is not uncommon to find great reliance being placed upon the rational strategy, apparently in line with the cultural faith in the "better mousetrap." This faith continues, despite the common experience that schools do not flock to accept a new innovation even when it is clearly superior to anything being used. Other common single-strategy approaches being advocated include the development of self-actualizing systems — psychological strategy — or the use of legal mandates — authority strategy. Such single-strategy approaches are likely to be slow and ineffective.

Diffusion strategies also are often typically determined with no consideration about the condition in which the diffuser wishes to leave the adopter. This situation may arise, of course, because the diffuser acts as a mere huckster; hucksterism may "sell" the particular innovation being promoted but may leave the adopter with little residual propensity to adopt again. But even well-intentioned diffusers fail to understand that their strategies ought to be generated by a consideration of the adopter. What is it that the adopter should be able to do, to think, or to feel, as a result of having been exposed to a diffusion strategy? Is he to be better trained? More skillful? More knowledgeable? More open? Obviously the wise choice of a diffusion strategy would be considerably aided through careful attention to these factors.

Too, each strategy is subject to certain practical obstructions. The fact that one can formulate strategies consistent with different views that one might hold of the adopter is, of course, not an adequate assurance that the strategies will work in practice. Indeed, as it turns out, each of the seven strategies is subject to certain practical obstructions that prevent it from being as effective as theory would indicate or that militate against its feasibility.

For example, a rational strategy may fail because busy practitioners rarely have the time and energy to immerse themselves sufficiently in facts and data to be convinced of the efficacy of an innovation on its merits alone. An authority strategy may fail because the educational enterprise is so vast that mere token compliance with a mandated action is often sufficient to avoid negative sanction but not sufficient to produce a durable change.

Furthermore, existing agencies and mechanisms designed to carry out diffusion activities are typically constrained to use only a segment of the strategy spectrum. Very often these agencies and mechanisms cannot choose from the full array of available strategies but are constrained to use only certain strategies. For example, a regional educational laboratory, while able to use rational and psychological strategies, is hardly in a position to use an authority strategy. State departments of education, which have a near monopoly on the authority strategy, are not really in a position to use psychological strategies without risking charges of government manipulation.

Moreover, diffusion agents typically do not have a clear and explicit perception of the strategy they are following. Even if none of the difficulties noted above existed, diffusion activities would probably still not be very effective because diffusion agents have not understood the meaning of the term strategy nor have they identified the variety of strategies available to them in any operational terms. This lack of clear understanding is partly rooted in the confusion between strategies and techniques but stems mainly from the fact that clear analyses of diffusion phenomena do not exist.

Improvement of Diffusion

What must be done then to make this crucial area of change effective? If my analysis is correct, personnel concerned with diffusion must perform several steps to do an adequate job:

1. They must make a careful analysis of the nature of the potential adopters whose attitudes they want to change.

2. They must select a strategy or combination of strategies that is consistent with their analysis and takes account of

the state in which they wish to leave the adopter. In all cases strategies must enhance, rather than reduce, the adopter's propensity to innovate again.

3. They must select a strategy or combination of strategies consistent with the posture and capabilities of the agency they represent.

4. They must use techniques that are consistent with the strategy they employ. There is no point in quoting facts and figures if the only effective way to approach an adopter is to buy him.

PROGRESS THROUGH THE PROCESS OF CHANGE

I have tried to sketch for you my impressions of how well we are doing in relation to educational improvement. In doing so, some explanation of the change process and its successes and failures today was essential. My remarks may easily be interpreted as pessimistic and negative, for I have tended to focus on problems rather than on successes. However, the case is far from hopeless. Indeed, our progress over the last several years has been remarkable. Surely, if we accomplish as much over the next five years as we have accomplished over the last five, the schools of 1972, will be radically different and undoubtedly improved. It is true that the attainment of the goal of an equally excellent education for all will take prodigious effort from all of us at all levels, ranging from the most mundane practice to the most esoteric conceptualization, but even our attempts to attain such a lofty goal have made this the most exciting educational time that history has ever witnessed. The challenge is there; we need but meet it.

Installing an Innovation

Louis J. Rubin

IT HAS BEEN ALMOST A DECADE since the movement to reform public education, with its accompanying demand for change and innovation, reached perceptible proportions. Much has occurred in the intervening period. There has been a fundamental analysis of the ways in which teaching and learning are shaped by human ambitions and by the technology available to man. Fine minds have brought their sharpest talents to bear upon the problems of instruction. In one subject field after another, teaching ideas have been reappraised and updated. Now, as the light of the social sciences is beginning to illuminate our traditional attitudes about the social education of the child, the emerging curriculum — at least as it is written — is a high celebration of what the goals of human enterprise can be.

But the vagaries of progress being what they are, the solving of one problem invariably gives rise to new ones. Once assailed for their old-fashioned ways, schools are now in many instances rushing into new things largely because change has become the fashionable hallmark of the day. It is not that innovation is undesirable; indeed, the quest for better ways must be carried on far beyond the present state of affairs.

Some approaches to innovation, however, are undesirable. An innovation, once it has demonstrated its value, must be put to use in a rational manner. In the hands of a practitioner trained only in an old method, a new method clearly will fall short of its potential. The casual adding of newness — the specious use of innovative paint to make a blue program red — is to be deplored. So, too, is the contrived invention of gimmicks to create artificial differences. Also deplorable is the amateurish careless abuse of a worthwhile innovation through a wanton disregard for the requirements upon which its success depends.

Neither restlessness, tinkering, nor frenetic activity make for genuine improvement. Change and innovation must be ordered by informed judgment, by the fruits of sound reasoning, and by a clear sense of the way things are. Thus, we must direct our attention to the difficulties at the very heart of school improvement as we try to innovate.

Several reasons support this approach. First, most of the innovations that can make an authentic difference to schools necessitate the retraining of instructional personnel, a phenomenon about which much too little is known, at least within the realistic constraints of the school world.

Second, the invention of innovations does not always parallel the school's needs. For example, if a given school suffers most from the inconsistencies of its instructional program, from the fuzziness of its teaching objectives, or from the dysfunction of its grading system, the adoption of a popular innovation probably will not remedy its basic ills. Unless a school has knowledge of its major weaknesses, it cannot select with intelligence from among the innovations available nor can it unleash with reasonable direction its own creative energy in solving problems. It is, therefore, important to find efficient procedures by which a school can accurately diagnose its weaknesses.

Third, little is known about the degree and kind of preparation that should precede the introduction of an innovation. In training teachers to use a new program, for example, how much of the training should deal with the program's theoretical underpinnings and how much with the classroom techniques it requires? What kind of training should occur before the innovation is introduced and what kind, after it is under way, when teachers can relate their training to an actual situation? What variations in training do different classes of innovation require?

Fourth, the innovative movement in education has become synonymous with the new subject curriculums and with a few well-publicized approaches to teaching such as flexible scheduling, team teaching, and various methods of individualizing instruction. These unquestionably merit the attention they have received, but their predominance has tended to obscure the value of other less well-known innovations and the need for local attempts to innovate in the solution of local problems. Of even greater importance, necessary school improvements are being overlooked in efforts to incorporate the more glamorous programs in the innovation mainstream.

Fifth, the strong emphasis upon change and innovation has important implications for the role of the school principal, the involvement of school faculties in instructional decisions, and the function of various outside agents in facilitating change.

THE CHANGE PROCESS

Various scholars have cataloged the change process in different ways, but most interpretations specify four basic phases. There is first a research phase in which worthwhile things are invented, either out of fresh insights or new combinations of old ingredients. Second, there is a development phase in which the products of research are packaged into operational procedures, tested in the field, modified, and generally made ready for dissemination. The assumption is that the development activity will produce a proven device for school improvement.

Third, there is a dissemination phase in which the developed programs are popularized through a number of activities. They can be advertised and marketed like cornflakes, they can be eulogized in professional journals, or they can be spread through interpersonal communication, a method that often leads to a stream of site visitations not unlike sight-seeing tours.

Fourth, there is an installation phase in which the innovation is introduced into the school program and nurtured until it becomes self-sustaining.

It is obvious that the four phases are subject to considerable overlap in actual practice. In the current press for school reform, we have not yet achieved a systematic procedure through which research, development, dissemination, and installation are assigned to the most appropriate agencies and through which an efficient transition from one phase to the next occurs. Research programs are fragmented, problems are considered in a piecemeal fashion, and the relationship between research and the real problems of schools often is no more than coincidental. As a case in point, organizations carrying out the development phase prefer, when additional basic research is needed, to perform their own investigations. Moreover, organizations are often fearful that other agencies will abuse their results and, as a consequence, tend to extend their own activity as much as possible. Thus, it is not uncommon to find a regional laboratory involved in all four phases of the change enterprise.

It seems to me that, at the moment, dissemination is less of a problem than the other three phases. This observation, of course, is qualified by the meaning I have assigned to dissemination. If one takes dissemination to mean something other than communication that makes a new program understandable to the profession at large, the observation becomes invalid. Spectacular new programs or brilliant new schooling techniques have not gone unheralded.

As the reform continues, dissemination may become more of a problem. For the present, at least, it is more likely that the mediocre will be praised than that the great will go unnoticed. The problems of the installation phase, on the other hand, are currently quite troublesome and should be considered before any suggestions about dissemination are introduced.

INNOVATION AND IMPROVEMENT

Experiments conducted at the Center for Coordinated Education (a school improvement venture at the University of California, Santa Barbara, supported by the Ford Foundation) suggest that schools install new programs for one of three reasons: (1) the program is clearly better than what it replaces, (2) the program is sufficiently popular that its absence is regarded as a sign of decadence, rigidity, or both, and (3) the program will enhance the school's image as a progressive institution.

It is unnecessary to labor the fact that irrational approaches to innovation create a number of problems. Frequently, for example, a new program is operated in a shoddy manner, or its intent is distorted so that the innovation's potential is distilled and sometimes destroyed. The notion of trial-testing an innovation, admittedly a useful technique, can become an excuse to launch a dozen dramatic innovations at the same time in the same school. On the basis of our experiments, I am convinced that a school can only deal with a limited number of innovations at any one time. Of greatest significance, however, a spurious approach to innovation ensures that there will be little connection between the school's instructional problems and the innovations introduced. In short, innovation and improvement are related, but they certainly are not the same.

To put the matter more pointedly — a bad school will never become good if it does no more than introduce popular innovations. It may have bad grading procedures, it may suffer from low morale, its administration may be simple-minded, or its teachers may be hampered by excessive student discipline problems. None of these problems can be corrected by PSSC, BSCS, IPI, or any other fashionable product in the innovation supermarket, their inherent worth notwithstanding. It is to be hoped that schools will come to view innovation as a necessary but insufficient part of improvement. There must be a rational effort to capitalize on the new, but there must be an equally rational effort to search out the inadequate and to apply correctives, even if the correctives are one, five, or ten years old.

THE PROCESS OF INSTALLING INNOVATIONS

The effective installation of an innovation in a school requires three sequential operations, each involving a number of discrete steps: preliminary analysis, strategy selection, and action.

Preliminary Analysis

The preliminary analysis serves several important functions. First, it creates a bridge between the introduction of an innovation and the improvement of the school. Second, it yields clues that are of considerable value in the strategy selection and action operations. Third, it provides at least a partial basis for determining which of the available innovations is most appropriate to the particular prevailing conditions.

The preliminary analysis operation consists of four steps: diagnosis of a weakness, analysis of the responsible factors, comparison of alternative correctives, and selection of the best corrective. In general, the preliminary analysis serves to draw the attention of school personnel to a specific problem, to the elements that create the problem, and to a number of different ways of overcoming the problem. It also provides a basis for selecting the best corrective option.

The first of the four steps, diagnosing a weakness, seems to be the most difficult. What a school staff perceives to be a major weakness depends upon its value system, its commitment, and its sense of purpose. Moreover, the job expectations of the individual teacher are often in conflict with the expectations of the school as an organization. The school, for example, may seek to produce a creative, self-directive child, while a given teacher may seek to produce a child who manifests obedience and self-control. Moreover, the machinations of mankind are such that almost any system can be made to work if enough compensating mechanisms are used, and it is often exceedingly difficult to persuade a faculty that its methods are inefficient, that its aspirations are short-sighted, or that its results are unimpressive.

Strategy Selection

The selection of an installing strategy is based upon three questions: (1) "What kind of an innovation is to be installed?" (2) "Who will engineer the installation?" and (3) "What conditions characterize the target environment?"

The most pervasive and most damaging myth associated with innovation lies in the assumption that all innovations can be introduced in the same way. When one wishes to introduce an innovation in subject matter, one plays a different game from that played when one wishes to introduce an innovation in teaching method. Innovations in the organization of the school are still another game. Similarly, strategies for installing an innovation differ when the individual engineering the change is powerful and inside the organization, powerful and outside the organization, powerless and inside the organization, and powerless and outside the organization. Some situations are susceptible to strong political influence from the community, others are not. Some teaching staffs are cohesive and manifest considerable group solidarity; others defer to the individuality and autonomy of each staff member.

Put succinctly, the purpose of the strategy selection operation is to gather evidence that will permit the installing agent to play his cards as well as he can. The more evidence the better. Differences among faculties are very great. The decision to use a direct (hard sell) approach as opposed to an indirect (soft sell) approach, for example, depends on the nature of the innovation, the talents of the installing agent, and the idiosyncrasies of the particular circumstance. There seems to be little doubt that every school staff has a definitive personality and that different staffs respond to different influence tactics.

It is obvious that considerable change will take place in the public school, whether or not deliberate interventionist tactics are employed. However, to the extent that educational leadership seeks to encourage and enhance the rate and quality of change, strategy selection is an important step. As we learn more about resistance to change and about the comparative benefits of various models of influence, strategy will become even more important.

Action

The action operation represents the culmination of the process. There are seven steps in this operation:

1. Analysis of the innovation's requirements in training, materials, and linkage to existing system.
2. Initiation of motivating pressures through inducing dissatisfaction and illuminating the rewards.
3. Initiation of the influence strategy.

4. Initiation of preparatory activities.
5. Installing the innovation.
6. Supporting the transition from old to new.
7. Linking the innovation to the permanent system.

The action operation is a logical sequence of steps leading to the adaptation of the innovation to the school's situation and, ultimately, to its permanent establishment in the program. It is important to note that the action operation does not begin until a specific weakness has been identified, the target environment has been analyzed, various solutions to overcoming the weakness have been considered, and a rational selection of an innovation has occurred.

The order of the first four steps is not significant. The attention devoted to each varies with the nature of the innovation and the character of the situation. The purpose of the seven steps is most easily depicted by a parallel list:

1. The staff must understand the innovation, its requirements, and its relation to the school's objectives.
2. The benefits of the innovation must be clear.
3. Specific strategies must be used to induce the staff to accept the innovation.
4. A "getting ready" program must be provided.
5. The innovation must be introduced.
6. Various kinds of support must be provided in order to prevent premature, or transitional, failure.
7. The innovation must be tied to the over-all program.

THE MATTER OF DISSEMINATION

Another important phase of the change process is dissemination. The purpose of dissemination is to make the consumer aware of a new way of doing something. Insofar as dissemination is principally a communication process, the problem is not new, and there are a number of established techniques. Indeed, some of the techniques are as old as man's effort to sell new products in the marketplace. At the risk of over-simplification, one can say that dissemination uses two primary devices: mass communication and interpersonal contact. The former is illustrated by the methods used to merchandise textbooks, and the latter by the spread of a new idea from district to district or school to school.

There are a number of difficulties associated with the dissemination of educational innovations. The provisions of projects funded under Title III of the Elementary and Secondary Education Act and other experimental projects normally do not permit sufficient time, energy, and money for dissemination activity. Since innovative behavior is highly prized, most people would rather invent their own miracles than import them from the outside. Furthermore, the dissemination of a new idea is always a long-range program. Most experimental projects terminate long before effective dissemination can take place. Moreover, many experimental projects are so restricted in their scope that a solid treatment of the research and development requirements is impossible. Such projects may result in worthwhile ideas, but they cannot result in tested innovations. Finally, many experimental projects are not tested in a variety of real environments. Their general applicability, as a consequence, is quite limited.

Apart from the remediation of these difficulties, several suggestions can be made. Let us assume that a school district has developed a solution to a problem. Let us further assume that it has both the desire and the means to spread its gospel. The program should then give consideration to certain facts about dissemination. For one thing, most inventions are of significance to a relatively select group. Reading teachers, for example, tend to be interested in reading methods rather than in administrative procedures. The dissemination program should, therefore, focus upon the appropriate consumer. If the innovation has undergone an authentic program of development and if it has been tested and refined, the inventors will know a great deal about the way it can most intelligently be used. The dissemination activities should then acquaint the potential consumer with the innovation's advantages and disadvantages and with the time, money, and transition requirements it imposes upon the consumer.

Only in some cases should the dissemination activity go beyond mere information. In short, dissemination must first inform the potential consumer; second, it must train the committed consumer. A district should familiarize a great many individuals with an innovation. Training in greater depth, however, should be restricted to individuals who will actually install the program.

The educator must remember also that people tend to communicate best at peer levels: board members are influenced by other board members, principals by other principals, and teachers by other teachers. Therefore, dissemination activities should take place on a variety of levels. It is also true that many projects are valuable even if the notions being tested prove to be unworkable. It is essential to distinguish between a quality project and a successful one. The failures, as well as the successes, of experimental projects are valuable coin for dissemination.

Finally, the educator must realize that in some instances dissemination should be an integral part of the project from its inception. For example, when the experiment deals with a process that is likely to be used in other situations, continuous dissemination is desirable. In other instances, when the experiment seeks a product, dissemination should be delayed until a useful procedure has been acquired.

A RATIONAL APPROACH TO CHANGE

The key to effective dissemination, as well as to installation and the whole concept of innovation, is to approach it rationally. A rational approach to dissemination necessitates analyzing the established techniques of dissemination and then adapting them to the particular educational system in terms of the consumers to be reached, the variety of levels, and the appropriate point at which to begin dissemination. The problematic process of installation also demands a rational approach, one that includes preliminary analysis and strategy selection before operation. And most importantly, innovation itself must be considered rationally in light of the particular needs and circumstances of each school. Otherwise the changes that could result in substantial educational improvement may only result in chaotic confusion and dismal failure.

Creative Directions for Innovation by Governments, Universities, and Industry

OVERVIEWS

A CHALLENGE TO INNOVATE
  Patsy T. Mink, *Democratic Congresswoman from Hawaii*

LIGHTHOUSES OF INNOVATION
  Harold Howe, II, *U. S. Commissioner of Education*

THE /I/D/E/A/ PLAN FOR INNOVATIVE SCHOOLS
  Eugene Howard, *Director*
  Innovation Dissemination, /I/D/E/A/

SCIENCE PLUS INNOVATIVE EDUCATIONAL ENVIRONMENT
  David Krech, *Department of Psychology*
  University of California at Berkeley

Overviews

A CHALLENGE TO INNOVATE
Patsy T. Mink

The federal government has merely scratched the surface in providing varied aid to education through the Elementary and Secondary Education Act. The government must continue to be a moving force in equalizing educational opportunities and seeking quality and freshness in the educational process. In concert with the states and local administrators, it must propose goals and directions for the effective use of new technology in education.

But educators, as experts in their field, must be the ones to take the lead and strike out on new paths. Congress can only respond. Unfortunately, many educators have been too timid in their applications of federal aid; they have used government funds to do more of the same rather than to improve and innovate.

The present approaches to education must be modernized and updated. Moreover, educators must seek new solutions in their exploration of these more urgent educational needs: improving the social status of the classroom teacher; creating new kinds of community surroundings through educational parks; strengthening the interaction between state and local jurisdictions and the federal government; disseminating weaknesses and strengths of diverse systems and techniques; and, most importantly, seeking to fullfill and develop each individual as a whole man.

LIGHTHOUSES OF INNOVATION

Harold Howe, II

Keen competition for funds under Title III of the Elementary and Secondary Education Act assures that educational change has the necessary element of quality. Competition is the element in ESEA Title III projects that produces the brightness of the beacons of these lighthouses of innovation.

Though a lighthouse is not needed in every school system, one should be visisble to every school. True innovation occurs very rarely, but new experiences and opportunities for people in different locations are as valuable as change that is unprecedented.

ESEA Title III gives educators the option of controlling the forces of change. Through this program, educators can direct change. In considering direction, there are several areas of concern that are of primary importance: suceeding with unsuccessful children, exploring solutions to the problems of racial isolation in the cities, reaching outside of the school to improve the process of education, developing teaching that actually changes behavior, and evaluating programs effectively through the introduction of independent elements.

THE I/D/E/A PLAN FOR INNOVATIVE SCHOOLS

Eugene Howard

The classroom must be the major target for stimulating true innovation, for too often a hard core of conventional practices lies beneath the surface of innovation. Many innovations mainly involve sheer label-switching. If innovation is to amount to something more than this, it must involve change in what students do when they learn, in what teachers do when they teach, and in what they both do when they interact with one another. Critical thinking, inquiry, and self-directiveness must be made a part of the curriculum.

The school of the future, according to the I/D/E/A plan, must be a self-evaluating structure that enables students to make meaningful decisions about their own learning by exercising well-defined options built into the curriculum. In this inquiry-centered school, the teacher would function as a stimulator, diagnostician, presenter, environment planner, and materials organizer. The student would function as an inquirer, object manipulator, idea organizer, explorer of curious phenomena, generalizer, discusser, and communicator of ideas and conclusions. With a built-in machinery for self-renewal, such a school would be receptive to change and would be changing as a result of critical thinking of staff and students, not as a result of the latest band wagon going by.

SCIENCE PLUS INNOVATIVE EDUCATIONAL ENVIRONMENT

David Krech

"Richard needs a bit more of an immediate-memory stimulator; Martha could probably do with a chemical attention-span stretcher." Does this sound like science fiction? Not too far in the future, the use of drugs, coupled with an innovative educational environment, could be the key to the enhancement of learning ability in humans.

Chemical experiments with rats have demonstrated that educational stimulation results in the physical improvement of their brains, while a lack of it results in measurable, deteriorative changes in the brain's chemistry and anatomy. Other experiments have revealed that some drugs have an inhibiting or stimulating effect on the brain's ability to learn. What a drug does to a rat's brain chemistry, however, depends upon the initial status of that chemistry. That chemistry, in turn, reflects the rat's early psychological and educational environment.

In reference to human beings then, this means that the biochemist and the educator of the future might combine their skills and insights for the educational and intellectual development of the child.

A Challenge to Innovate

Patsy T. Mink

As A NATION we are now engaged in an aggressive program to improve the educational institutions of our country. In the historic 89th Congress, after long debate and struggle, we were finally able to enact the first massive program of general aid to elementary and secondary schools. It has always seemed to me to be an anomaly that we should have had to work so long and so assiduously to help education when, of all the institutions of civilized society, it is the only organized effort of man that truly epitomizes the democratic ideals of freedom and opportunity. The booklearning, the concepts and principles of freedom, the mores and traditions of this union, the dreams and aspirations of our unspoiled youth, and the motivation to become a part of the complex mechanism of life reflect the values of a strong and vigorous educational system. I cannot conceive of any more vital concerns for the future of this nation than those that focus upon the quality of our education.

There are many who argue that the federal government has already moved too far and too quickly. My contention is that we have only scratched the surface, that far more needs to be done if we are really to meet the challenges of the future. Not only do we have to equalize the opportunities for educating all of our children, those in the ghettos and slums of our cities and those in the remote regions of the countryside without the wealth to sustain an adequate education, but we must constantly seek quality and freshness of approach.

It is in maintaining this delicate balance between controlling equality and innovation that the federal government meets its greatest challenge. It can be a moving force to expand opportunity for all our children, for no one would deny the fundamental premise that equal opportunity ought to be granted to all. At the same time it can be a force that innovates to help shape the education of the future.

Now that we have made an initial stride forward, much of our attention must be turned to modernizing, updating, and freshening our present approach to education. In two years of experience with the Elementary and Secondary Education Act (ESEA), we have learned that many educators have been too timid in their applications of federal aid; too often they have viewed government funds as a means to do more of the same, and too many have shied away from the implicit challenge to experiment, to revamp, and to innovate. We in Congress cannot reach into the individual classroom and define and create new programs that are needed. As educators, as experts in your field working with the human materials, it is you who must take the lead and strike out on the new paths changing times demand. Congress is not by nature a pioneering institution; it often moves cautiously, and it is often dilatory because of the very nature of its composition. The status quo always mounts a strong defense in our society, and we must devote our efforts to overcoming the prevalent "what was good enough for me is good enough for my kids" attitude. The stimulus for change must emanate from the classroom. It must be a constant flow of departure from the norm. Experimentation and innovation are key concepts and themes. Only by holding these as values can we hope to conquer the tremendous public and official inertia standing between us and our vision of the future.

With the passage of ESEA and additional funds allocated for research in education, it is quite obvious that the apparatus of education is a growing business demanding our attention. Corporations are keenly interested in the possibilities for new markets. New, exciting hardware has hit the streets; and educators have become intrigued, fascinated, and sometimes, perhaps, fearful of the implications. A new, mechanical, computerized industry offers interesting avenues for public investment. We no longer are talking only about individual teaching machines for classroom use but about programed research and reference facilities.

The development of such technology was inevitable, and the extent of its practical application must be confronted. We must examine these new teaching and research techniques and set the limits of public expenditure for such items, lest we move in directions that serve to compound the inequalities now making educational opportunity unattainable to the vast majority of our children. Just as man must set certain goals in life for himself, so it is imperative that we set goals for the machines we have created. The governments of nations have set up priorities with reference to international agreements on nuclear weaponry; our government, in concert with the states and with local school administrators, must similarly come to grips with proposing values for the new technology in education. By setting forth goals and ideals for the use and dissemination of technology, our nation can continue to foster and promote the goals of equal opportunity and avoid being the instrument for furthering a sophisticated inequality. Those who program the materials for use in these teaching machines will share a great responsibility for their effectiveness. Properly used, the machine will serve to relieve the classroom teacher of the monotony of the repetition and exercise that has been so much a part of the daily routine of teaching.

I am firmly convinced that the classroom teacher, the heart and head of our entire school system, has truly been the neglected and forgotten element. Not only is he in need of advice on new techniques and gadgetry, but his needs (and thereby his consequent effectiveness in nurturing our youth) must receive far more attention than is now given. We need to elevate the teacher in the public eye; we need to give him his deserved status. We must make him aware of how our hopes rise and fall with him; we must allow him the opportunity not only to teach but also to learn and to renew his knowledge and abilities. It is another anachronism of American education that the teacher, historically an honored figure treated with great respect by societies of many eras, should be so carelessly relegated to the status of tutor rather than mentor. Much remains to be done, legislatively and within the local community, to develop the education profession and its image.

There is also crying need for innovation and a new outlook in relation to the changing patterns of our social structure. We must develop a concern for creating new kinds of community surroundings. How, for example, are we to contend with the growth of the inner and outer city? How are we to provide for more meaningful and distributed urban growth and development? Here, too, we must break with tradition and establish centers of learning at the secondary level where students may come for the best we are able to offer. The concept of an educational park, drawing disparate communities of traditionally separated children into a common community, supports the concept of an organic society. It enhances *esprit de corps* or *communitas* as the Greeks once termed it. Built-in open spaces, with easy access through tunnels or overpasses, housing various kinds of activities from grade through high school to continuing education, the park defines more meaningfully what we intend when we speak of equalizing opportunity for all.

These parks would acknowledge the fact that our environment is a dynamic one, that there is interaction between the human being and his surroundings, and that there is a flow of interchange between man's internal and external existence. The phenomenal growth of the junior college and community college systems across the country can be regarded as a manifestation of our recognition of these dynamics, and we may well learn to apply what success we achieve through these institutions to our secondary schools in the future. There is a great need for an interaction between the states and local jurisdictions and the federal government; there is a need for pooling research capabilities and resources through data collection to quicken the pulse of education at all levels and in every part of the country. The weaknesses and strengths of diverse systems and techniques need to be recorded and analyzed and then disseminated for the benefit of all.

As we discuss and dissect the role of increasing specialization and advanced technology, we can perceive that the education industries are humane recognitions of the fact that engineering know-how can be harnessed for the general good of the populace. As it has always been when we have had to utilize our technological potential to tap the natural resources and wonders of our physical environment, so too, today, we seek to understand how the machine can help us learn and teach our children. And we must listen to those who voice concern about our massive attemtps to standardize education and reduce the individual to a by-product of cybernetics.

The tools of learning, fundamental though they be, ought always to be flexible; they ought to be tools as opposed to techniques. We must somehow prepare the student for his role, for the accelerating rate of change he will have to contend with and adjust to. Yet we must reveal to him that beneath the temporal nature of scientific and technological change exist more fundamental tools of existence out of which our past was made and from which our future can also be fashioned.

At a time when we are talking of nihilism and apathy, it becomes increasingly important to discuss the particularity of the individual, a thing in himself. Too frequently, and perhaps even inevitably, we are confronted with descriptive numbers; we find our lives arranged by systems we originally devised for our convenience. The individual seeks to simplify the clutter; he seeks to order, to shape, and to mold. At the same time his peculiarity causes bewilderment in a system; there seems little or no coherence in the pattern. The avenues the federal government has opened in education become more significant here, for the government is a human construction and has acted, and undoubtedly will continue to act, as a mirror of our ideals. Only if we truly believe and practice education as the renewal and perpetuation of a society, will the educative task become that of molding and shaping a future not yet in existence.

What, we might ask, are we doing to ensure that the monies we are spending for education are entering those areas that will produce men and women better able to meet the changing demands of a still undertermined future? In our own youth, none of us possessed the clairvoyance to predict life today with all its advances in technology and their impact on civilization. How much effort, then, are we now expending in an attempt to anticipate what will be the human and the educational problems of the 21st century? In our sometimes frenetic efforts to bring our schools into the second half of the 20th century, might it be asking too much to set our sights 50-to-a-100 years hence and attempt to forecast what life will be like then? Perhaps if we envision the future, we may move forward with conscious goals instead of always playing "catch-up."

And yet there are portents and signs of various afflictions besetting the human condition today that cannot help being magnified should we not take heed and apply the lessons available to us. I refer to the alienation of increasing numbers of our youth from traditional mores, rebels denying entrenched customs. As thousands and thousands of them flock toward the banners of dissent, to the cults of individuality, to what we disparagingly term hippie and beat behavior, we see more clearly that we have failed to channel and direct the restless, intelligent energies of many of our most promising young people. Bored and unfulfilled with the status quo we offer them, they call for massive innovation and shift in directions. I am convinced that we must respond to the message if we can but learn to interpret it. We must perceive our educational failures to date and face up to them if we are to ever begin the long hard road to the means and the methods of bringing out the best in every individual. The goals of education remain unchanged, yet we tend to forget that the development of the whole man is our lasting and intangible ideal.

We need to educate the whole person. To do this, we cannot focus just on partitioned academic subjects; we must also focus on the human personality. We must endeavor to create an appreciation for the human race as something special, to develop laughter, and to create a climate of compassion and tolerance where each child will come to understand his own emotions and his own mind. We must teach him to understand his own body, train his eye to see and his ears to hear, help him learn to jump and run, to throw a ball, to ride a bicycle, to lift a weight. All these are integral to the uniqueness of each of us as individuals. We must teach a youth how to value what is best in himself without scorning his peers, who may have other talents. Besides the specialized textbooks and techniques for honing the modern mind, we need to keep alive in our youth a love of music and art and an appreciation of theology and myth. We need to evoke mystery, wonder, and inquisitiveness about the natural world and our youngsters' relations to it.

The swirl of technology is so massive and confusing that we need to seek out and emphasize the fundamentals of human existence; we need to help our children sift out the important values in life. Even with the most advanced knowledge and the most sophisticated society, there exists the possibility that we neglect to educate our youth to develop an awareness of his fellow man; we neglect to educate him in the pursuit of happiness and self-fulfillment through meaningful and significant goals; we neglect to reveal to him the deep values of family and community living. If these ideals remain neglected, I submit we shall be reversing the processes of human evolution and destroying the bright promise with which each individual is brought forth into this exciting and often bewildering world.

Lighthouses of Innovation

Harold Howe, II

THAT THE FEDERAL GOVERNMENT would make available two hundred million dollars to local school districts on a competitive basis to effect creative change in education was a dream that no educator ever thought would become reality. But this dream did indeed come into being, and we are now looking forward to levels of investment in educational change by the federal government that none of us can foresee. Under Title III of the Elementary and Secondary Education Act, seventy-five million dollars were appropriated in the first year, which ended June 30, 1966, and one hundred thirty-five million dollars in the second. Now Congress has made available nearly two hundred nine million dollars for the present year, fiscal 1968. We are indeed on the way to receiving good support from the federal government for what school districts want to do to bring about change.

This is a totally new opportunity. Educators across the country are looking forward to entirely different options as a result of this action in the federal government.

What Title III is designed to produce is a series of light-houses around the land that people can look at and learn from. Though a lighthouse is not needed in every school system, every school should be able to see a lighthouse. It is these lighthouses that Title III is in the business of building, and competition is the element that produces the brightness of their beacons.

PROCESSES AND PROBLEMS OF TITLE III

The Idea of Change

This federal program is based on the idea of change, and change is perhaps a better word to use in reference to it than the word innovation. We should begin to think realistically about the distinction between innovation and change and realize that true innovation happens very seldom. It is very rare in the affairs of the world that any person or group of people really has a brand new idea. But there are all sorts of new experiences for people in places where there have been no opportunities and no adjustment to change. These people need to get ideas from other places and put them into operation at home.

Therefore, while we need to keep in mind the notion of innovation with reference to it, the Title III program should perhaps focus more on the concept of change. It should emphasize the means by which there can be new centers of different kinds of activity, of local activity, and of activity that has been demonstrated elsewhere, can be demonstrated again, and then carried on further. In this way the process of change goes on constantly, even though there is no notion of innovation in every single case.

Such demonstration is the technique on which the effectiveness of Title III activity really depends. Effectiveness also depends on dissemination about the success of a project; just as important is dissemination about failure of a project. Whenever we have change in which there is some element of innovation, people are sometimes going to fail. Dissemination of failure is, of course, a more difficult requirement because we educators seldom examine our failures honestly. We very rarely admit that something new we initiated has failed to work out or to produce what we expected and, therefore, should be abandoned.

A Percentage of Failures

If a program like Title III is going to operate over a period of time, there will be a regular percentage of failures. If there were not a percentage of failures, then the program itself would be a failure because people should be trying projects that are sufficiently on the frontiers to cause doubt about whether they will work out.

Those people who administer the program, the school boards that find new elements being brought into their schools, and the states that observe new excursions in different directions for teacher training, for example, should be willing to accept the notion of a reasonable percentage of failure, since any experiment that is a guaranteed success is not an experiment.

Competition

Another absolutely essential element of the Title III program is the competitive element. The successful applicants for Title III grants are those who first visualized something that was important for them to do. They then looked at the needs of their schools, at the priorities among those needs, and prepared and submitted a proposal to be part of a competition. When these proposals reached the U.S. Office of Education, competent educators in the country were brought in to study them. The proposals numbered two or three times the total amount of money available for Title III.

This kind of competition always creates tension, and this type of tension is constructive. Necessarily some projects are rejected, and because of this competition, the quality of the proposals that are approved is better. If the federal government is going to invest money in encouraging change, then it must make sure that the nature of change has an element of quality about it. Only competition can guarantee that. If Title III ever becomes a program of grants that every school district has a right to receive, then it will not produce quality change.

Therefore, we need to seek ways to bring about a national competition for excellence. One possibility I would oppose is that the Office of Education be the grand arbiter of all these matters. The Office of Education is not the grand arbiter of them now; it provides a middleman service. Through this service, it brings into consultation about Title III projects the most competent and authoritative persons in the United States to read proposals, to make judgments and recommendations about them, and eventually to influence whether or not certain types of proposals are to be funded.

Duplication

The problem of duplication also enters into the process. We need a national clearinghouse in which authoritative persons provide the services. We need persons who are not bureaucrats in Washington but are from the field — the colleges, the universities, and the schools — to look at the extent of investment under a program for change in various categories. There should be a reasonable level of investment in various kinds of activities, such as improving curriculums, training teachers, using equipment, and looking at some of the major issues in education in the planning of programs. There needs to be a reasonable balance across the United States in addressing ourselves to these problems as Title III moves ahead.

TITLE III MAJOR AREAS OF CONCERN
Succeeding with the Unsuccessful

While no one could set down in only five or six different topics the particular kinds of concerns that ought to be given priority in Title III investment, there are some areas that should attract the major interests of persons concerned with Title III.

The first area of concern is really directly related to the major purposes of the Elementary and Secondary Education Act under Title I. This is the question of how to succeed with the children who are failing in the schools.

We used to say that the children themselves were to blame for failure. Most of us now realize that there may be things the schools could do and have not done. There may be services they could offer. There may be types of organization. There may be methods of teaching. There may be subtle attitudinal relationships between staff and student that will aid in producing success instead of failure.

Exploration of this whole area is of primary importance, for this is the main business of school — enabling children to be successful. To some extent, the schools of the United States have not been about that business but have been instead acting as a sorting device to decide which children should be rejected from the schools. A fair proportion of them, of course, have been rejected. We still have a million high school dropouts a year. It is to that group and the misfortunes they have, the frustrations they face, and the kinds of lives they are going to lead in the future that a significant proportion of Title III investment should be addressed.

There is a very real opportunity for a school district to combine the federal funding it is eligible to receive under Title I of the Elementary and Secondary Education Act, which gives aid for special programs for educationally deprived children, with the federal funding it might seek under Title III of that Act. There has not been nearly enough exploration of building combinations across those two titles. There has been a good deal more exploration of building combinations between Title III of the Elementary and Secondary Education Act and the funding available there under Title IV, the research title of the Act. School systems should try to coordinate Title III and Title I.

This has not been neglected altogether; there are some very adventurous explorations with Title III funds on behalf of disadvantaged youngsters, for example, the planning grants that have gone to some of the big cities. These look forward to such issues as the location of their schools, their size, their reaction to the new notion about the educational park, and the shape of the construction for the school system in the future. These kinds of explorations are directly related to opportunities for disadvantaged children.

There also has not been as much exploration in the realm of vocational education through Title III as there should be. There is a great need for adventurous exploration of how this group of a million children who are dropping out of high school every year with no entry job skills available to them could be served with job skills. The Title III projects designed for that purpose should be more numerous. Partly because they seem less numerous than they should be, a proposal has been made in Congress that, if adopted, will create a kind of small-scale Title III directly related to vocational education with a fund of thirty million dollars. This program would be specifically focused on the problems of vocational education and of innovation and change in vocational education.

Racial Isolation

The second issue, which is directly related to the first, is solving the problems of racial isolation in our cities. Quite a number of Title III projects have developed around this prickly problem, and anyone who becomes involved in it through a Title III project is going to awaken all sorts of concerns in his community. He is going to find himself suffering the usual sufferings of the innovator, only he is going to suffer more. The innovator is a person who is not accepting the immediate ruts that exist. He is jumping out of them, going off in another direction, and therefore exposing everybody in the ruts to the possibility that he might be wrong. This just annoys the people in the ruts. It annoys them a great deal, particularly when the innovator jumps out of the rut with the idea of doing something about the problem of racial imbalance and racial isolation — working on issues of who goes to school with whom, and trying to show that it is important for different kinds of people from different backgrounds, different races, and different strata to go to school together. When you start promulgating that kind of idea, it becomes unpopular, not only because it is an innovation but because it strikes at the heart of many, many attitudes that are very deeply held, although not very often admitted. It is important that the people engaged in educational change have the courage to pick up this particular thorny problem and develop related projects.

It is a great credit to the educational agencies in those cities and towns that are using various funds available under Title III to work on this particularly difficult set of problems. Incidentally, this set of problems does not confine itself just to the big cities. It exists in a variety of ways throughout the country. There is increasing concern in the Office of Education, for example, about bilingual education and the problems of Mexican-American children in the Southwest, the French-speaking children in northern Maine, and other minority groups who really require educational change on their behalf if they are not to become dropouts from the schools.

Reaching Outside the School

The third area in which Title III is performing well and in which there should be additional energy is how to enlist the forces outside the school on behalf of education. Our generation of educators has come to the conclusion that the schools cannot do the job of educating children alone and that we have to enlist outside forces. We start by using various kinds of electronic and other media to bring those forces into the school. But we use much more imaginative approaches when we move children around communities, use other institution arrangements within communities, and involve businesses, museums, and libraries that are in the community in a variety of new relationships with the school. One of the great virtues of Title III is that it encourages such action.

People who have responsibility for projects under Title III should ask themselves the question, "What is there about the project I now am operating that could be improved to make it better for the children, the teachers, or the parents involved? Would it be better if I were to rethink its community involvement, if I were to look around this area to see what is available that would somehow bring a new and richer cross-current into the project we have in mind?" We are really going through a revolution in this respect, and it is very much to the credit of projects operating across the country that the schools have opened their doors and are beginning to welcome all kinds of people. New types of personnel are coming into the schools very rapidly. It was only five or six years ago that the teacher's aide was really an innovation. School administrators are now beginning to think about how to use other kinds of people from various business, professional, and other areas in the school to stimulate the teaching and learning. Such projects are extremely worthwhile.

Changing Behavior

One area that is not considered very much is developing teaching that actually changes behavior. We need some responsible exploration of this. We go along naively assuming that we can change people by giving them courses in certain areas. We have courses in driver training to make better drivers. We are beginning to think about courses in human development, in sex, and in marriage because we think that we can thus solve the problems of divorce and help young people with some of the frustrations and disappointments that so many of them are confronting so early nowadays. We introduce courses in citizenship that are reaching toward changes in attitudes and changes in behavior. But we need more exploration of the degree to which formal learning, as it is usually presented in the school, really does have an influence on behavior and on attitudes.

Several years ago someone surveyed the attitudes of the teenage generation on the Bill of Rights in the United States Constitution. It was a very interesting survey, which revealed that a frighteningly large proportion of teenagers who had studied the Bill of Rights in the Constitution and who knew about what the declaration of those rights says about the individual's protection against arbitrary authority, really believed that people should not necessarily be accorded those rights, particularly if they were from minority groups.

These kinds of attitudes we seek to influence through course instruction in the school, but it is questionable whether we are attaining the desired objective. This raises the whole question of developing experiments under Title III that bring a different relationship among the people who are in the school so that perhaps by living together in a different way in the school, we might have some influence over attitude. How can we develop citizenship and how can we develop an individual who is a good citizen when the teacher is not around?

Some Title III projects should address themselves to this subtle, elusive, and difficult problem of building proper behavior, sensible attitudes, and a dedication to the best that is American in the children in our schools. Projects could do this perhaps not by teaching students about these areas; a mathematics teacher who has the right relationship to his mathematics class can probably build a lot more constructive attitudes then a civics teacher who has a highly authoritarian relationship to his civics class. There are not many Title III efforts in this area. This is one of the most difficult problems to solve, but someone should pay attention to it.

Evaluation

Another area that has been neglected by developers of Title III projects is evaluation. This year the Office of Education has been trying to transmit to its programs the significance of evaluation. It is true that it is extremely hard to evaluate a project that is just in the process of getting started and is only a year-and-a-half old. It certainly is frustrating when political figures and other people want to know from us educators exactly what progress is being made. They ask, "Haven't you evaluated? After all, it has been in existence for a year. What are you producing?" We know that children are not changed in a year. Indeed, in five, six, or eight years it is hard to tell whether they have been changed very much. We do encounter difficulty with evaluation, and yet we have to have built into every project and into every major program some effort at evaluation.

However, it is true that there is a necessary conflict between innovators and evaluators. There should be. One of the dangers of a program like Title III is that the innovators will capture the evaluators, and then we will never know what happened. We need to find ways to set up systems for evaluation so that we have some professional skeptics around, people who aren't all caught up with the enthusiasm of the project, who are looking at it with a cold, fishy eye and saying, "Why are you doing that? What is it proving? Have you thought of testing out this way of evaluating that particular part of your program?" Planning evaluation that includes an independent element should be encouraged.

There are no Title III projects in which a local school district has invited a neighboring school district to evaluate its project. That would be an interesting approach. There probably is a certain amount of jealousy in a neighboring school district because the other fellow got the grant, and so they would be good evaluators. We should be thinking of this type of evaluation of Title III projects.

A CHANCE TO CONTROL CHANGE

As I look at this whole program, my belief is that if it is successful and if it expands, it allows us to do something we otherwise never would have had a chance to do. It gives us the option of controlling the change that takes place, rather than letting it happen to us.

There are a great many forces working on the schools, forces so powerful that we cannot control them, but we can do something about the adjustment of the schools to those forces. These forces are the obvious ones — the development of new knowledge, the development of new technology and means of teaching and learning, the changes in the economy that require different skills of people as they go into jobs, and the adjustments of the schools concerning such people so that they will have those different skills.

These forces are the requirements of a society that is beginning to act as if it wanted to do the things it said it believes. We have said a lot of things in the United States about the equality of people in this country, and now the society is beginning to do something about the equality of people in a very dramatic way. Unless the schools make the changes that bring about that equality in the schools, society will be forced to do so by outside elements. The Title III program gives us a chance to work on these elements of change as responsible educators; it is a chance we certainly should not miss. Fortunately today there are those who are already doing this job and have not missed that significant opportunity to change the schools and, by doing so, to change the world.

The I/D/E/A Plan for Innovative Schools

Eugene Howard

"THE MORE THINGS CHANGE, the more they stay the same," goes the old French proverb. This saying applies very aptly to much of what is termed innovation in our rapidly changing schools. Scratch the surface of what a principal tells you is an innovation and you are likely to find a hard core of conventional practices. There is a lot of superficial, under-planned, under-organized, under-financed, and under-staffed innovation going on.

Team teaching, for example, too often turns out to be a re-organization of mediocrity — teachers doing together the kind of teaching that should not be done at all. Flexible scheduling, when examined closely, often means the substitution of a computer-built rigidity for a hand-built one. Independent study in many instances turns out to be a plan for allowing students to do their homework in the cafeteria; in other cases it becomes a plan for allowing students choices of ways in which they may be coerced.

Seminars often have become small classes devoted to the sharing of prejudice and ignorance among students, or worse, a means whereby the teacher can teach conventionally smaller groups of students. Architects are designing so-called innovative buildings that group conventional classrooms in circles and hexagons instead of in rectangles. Innovation in curriculum typically means that the teachers have been permitted to adopt the newest form of rigidity conceived by a group of scholars sitting on a campus somewhere. Educational television as an innovation has been used to impose an electronic lock-step on the student partially to replace the teacher-built lock-step of the past.

These comments on team teaching, independent study, flexible scheduling, newly designed buildings, and seminar instruction do not indicate opposition to innovations. What is objected to is the use of these labels as substitutes for meaningful change. The purpose is to illustrate that the more things change, the more they stay the same.

This is the age of the easy solution to the complex problem. It is the age of instant coffee and tea, instant TV dinners, and instant innnovators. The instant innovator can be defined as an educator who wants to do things differently without really changing anything. His principal method is the technique of label-switching — the pinning of an innovative label onto an obsolete practice.

DIFFERENCES BETWEEN SUPERFICIAL AND BASIC CHANGE

Change in education does not have to be superficial. It can be basic and meaningful; it can mean a change in learner and teacher roles. It can be a change based on information instead of prejudice; it can be a change based on a thoughtful analysis of a situation instead of an intuition or expediency. Systematically planned trial and error must, in our innovative schools, replace capricious trial and error.

Suppose principals were immediately able to cause the following organizational changes: the development of a new organizational plan for the school that placed every teacher on a teaching team, the addition of noncertified instruction assistants and clerical assistants to the staff, and the redesigning of the school plant, which replaced the 900-square-foot class-rooms with large, open spaces labeled "learning laboratories," and provided special facilities for independent study and small-group instruction. What has been accomplished? It is now possible for innovation to take place in the school? What hasn't been done?

1. What learners do when they learn, or what teachers do when they teach have not been affected.
2. The content of the curriculum has not been altered.
3. The teachers have not broken the lock-step, and the implementation of a continuous-progress curriculum has not occurred, though both are organizationally possible.
4. A program of independent study has not been developed.
5. The use of teachers of the seminar method to stimulate critical and analytical thinking has not begun.

Thus, there is an important difference between superficial change and basic change. Organizational innovation will not by itself solve nonorganizational problems.

Innovation, if it is to amount to something more than mere organizational manipulation, must involve a change in what teachers do when they teach, what students do when they learn, and what they both do when they interact with one another.

COERCION IN THE SCHOOLS

For students, the three R's of restraint, rote memory, and regurgitation must be replaced by inquiry-centered activities — activities that help students to ask meaningful questions about real situations in which they find themselves, to seek information on which to base conclusions, to act on the basis of the conclusions reached, and to evaluate the results of the action in relation to the predicted outcomes. Critical thinking, inquiry, and self-directiveness must be made a part of the curriculum.

Our schools, typically, have not been organized in such a way as to encourage this kind of activity on the part of students — or teachers either for that matter. Rather they are designed to serve the needs of the bright conformists, those students and teachers who get their kicks out of doing things the way they are told to do them. Our schools need to be made safe for the nonconformist, the divergent thinker, and the creative teacher and student who prefer to have something to say about what, how, when, and where they will learn.

Have you ever stopped to think that the typical student in our coercion-centered schools today has almost nothing to say about what he will learn, how he will learn it, who will help him learn it, where he will go to learn it, what materials he will use, how long he will take at the task, or how he will be evaluated? The most important decisions regarding learning are made for the student by rigid schedules, rigid curricula, rigid buildings, rigid principals, and rigid teachers. Then we wonder why we can't motivate more students to learn. The time has come for us to declare war against coercion in our schools. Coercion should be made obsolete because it does not work with a large percentage of our students.

INQUIRY-CENTERED SCHOOLS OF THE FUTURE

The school of the future should be a well-structured school, but its structure should be designed to free people, not to confine or unduly restrict them. I am not advocating a sloppy school or a school lacking structure; rather, I am promoting a school that has built into it a new kind of structure that enables students to make meaningful decisions about their own learning through exercising well-defined options that have been built into the curriculum.

Also, the innovative school of the future should be a self-evaluating school. It should be a school where teachers and students evaluate the result of their actions on the basis of factual information. It should be a school where questions are carefully phrased so that information pertinent to the question can be obtained. It should be a school where action is based on such information instead of on prejudice, conjecture, or expediency, as is the case in most schools today. It should be a school in which the teacher functions as a stimulator, diagnostician-prescriber, environment planner, and materials organizer. It should be a school where the student functions as an inquirer, an object manipulator, an idea organizer, an explorer of curious phenomena, a generalizer, a discusser, and a communicator of ideas and conclusions.

Such a school would be receptive to innovation and change because it would have the machinery for self-renewal built into its structure; but it would be changing as a result of thoughtful, critical thinking by the staff and students, not as a result of the latest band wagon that might be going by. Its changes would be tailored uniquely for that school's students, teachers, and community. Principals could come and go, and the change process would continue because the process would not depend upon the charisma of any one person to sustain it. The "boom and bust" phenomena, now a characteristic disease of our country's innovative schools, would no longer plague us.

We refer to such a school as an inquiry-centered school. It is a major purpose of I/D/E/A's (Institute for the Development of Educational Activities) demonstration-schools project to stimulate the development of a small number of such schools.

To encourage the demonstration schools to develop in this direction, we use primarily what Egon Guba has labelled a "psychological strategy." Once the school is committed to the inquiry concept, I/D/E/A supports the personnel in the school as they seek to adapt the concept to their own particular situation. I/D/E/A relies primarily on the diffusion techniques of helping, involving, and intervening, rather than on showing or telling.

I/D/E/A DEMONSTRATION SCHOOLS

As a method of intervening, we are placing three additional faculty members in each of the 36 schools in the demonstration-schools project: a teacher-researcher to stimulate the faculty to make decisions rationally in accordance with information rather than expediency; a disseminator to help others understand and, perhaps, adopt some of the innovative practices at work in the school; and a community-school man to involve the community meaningfully in the developmental process to assure continued community support for the innovative program. These three persons, together with the principal and other selected change agents in the school, form what has been termed a development team — a group of leadership people on the school staff dedicated to fostering a process of inquiry in the school as decisions are made regarding teaching and learning.

The concept of the change agent in the school is not a new one. It has been advocated by Matthew Miles, Art Gallaher, Richard Carlson, and many other students of the change process. J. Lloyd Trump is just completing a nation-wide experiment in the utilization of administrative interns as change agents in schools. The I/D/E/A/ concept of a change agent differs principally from that described by others in that it utilizes not an individual but a team of leaders in the school as facilitators of the change process.

It also differs from previously suggested models in that it is used primarily in schools that have already made broad school-wide organizational changes. They have already installed flexible schedules; they have already provided for flexible use of facilities; they have already made at least a commitment toward adopting a flexible, open-ended, continuous-progress curriculum. They have, to a large extent, cleared away the organizational debris that impedes thoughtful and meaningful change in most schools, and they are now ready to turn their attention to the development of new roles for learners, teachers, and administrators.

I/D/E/A/ is working with 36 of the nation's most innovative schools, helping them to achieve excellence and helping them to become more influential. Many of these schools have already received a great deal of publicity, and all of them are engaged in systematic dissemination activities. I/D/E/A and ESEA Title III are helping these schools improve both evaluation and dissemination so that each one of the 36 schools in the network becomes a change agent, stimulating innovative activities in hundreds of other schools in all parts of the country.

A new kind of national organization is emerging, an organization dedicated to systematically fostering thoughtful evaluation and innovation in our nation's schools. We are encouraging these schools to disseminate information about innovative practices, not just someone's opinion; and we are encouraging the schools to carefully evaluate those practices that are being disseminated. But we are also doing something else. Some of the schools are disseminating not only promising practices but also processes. Probably the question most commonly asked by visitors to these schools is, "How do you persuade a faculty to make changes such as this?" or "How can I get things moving in my school?" The demonstration schools are now implementing and will be disseminating new processes for stimulating thoughtful change within the school. This change process, when put in motion in a school desiring to move away from conventional practices, will help the school in a systematic manner.

We believe that dissemination — whether it be of practices or processes — is a very personal thing. This is why the consortium of demonstration schools is not only a communications network but also a working group. Teachers learn about continuous progress, for example, not by hearing lectures on the subject but by working with teachers from other schools on building modular units of instruction. We believe that teachers learn best from other teachers and administrators from other administrators. The demonstration-schools project is a group of avant-garde schools that share common purposes and learn from one another by exchanging ideas, people, and publications.

MUCH REMAINS TO BE DONE

Most of our schools are obsolete, engaging in many medieval practices that are actually harmful to children. Momism and apron-stringism are running rampant in our elementary schools, alienating boys from academic pursuits at an early age. This little-flower approach to education is especially destructive in such areas as art and literature.

The forces of anti-intellectualism are still great in our schools. All too often these forces are led by the principal himself, who has come to his job via the athletic director route. Such a principal tries to run his school the way he used to run his athletic program — with the gym in the forefront and the rest of the school as an annex.

On the other hand, our profession is plagued with intellectual snobs. Their Phi Beta Kappa keys dangling from their tie clasps, they seek to insure the respectability of their subjects by designing courses appropriate only for the select few.

Too much of the content of our courses, at all levels, is composed of fragments of information unrelated to one another and unrelated to reality as perceived by the student. The curriculum lacks unity, order, and sequence, without which the student becomes confused and ineffective. Teachers don't understand that a grasp of the structure of a subject is essential to understanding its content in depth.

Our schools are plagued with authoritarianism and rigidity. This authoritarianism is characterized by formal delegation of authority to appointed leaders, rigid, complex, heirarchical organization patterns, formal lines of communication operating within well-marked channels, watchdog-like supervision of teachers, and the reward and coercion method of inducing change. Such organizations and their resulting climates of fear and hostility are best calculated to serve the interests of mediocrity.

Too many philosophies of education are formulated by committees, only to be filed and forgotten. Too many schools truly do not stand for anything positive in education that has been translated into the attitudes of people and the content of curricula. Irrational grouping practices are still the rule, and our profession is currently divided over which irrational grouping plan is best. Too many so-called innovations are superficial in nature and are under-staffed, under-planned, under-evaluated, and under-financed.

A great deal remains to be done. In the typical community, there are only two places where a resident of 1920 would feel perfectly at home — the railroad station and the school. Where's the method? How do we begin? We are suggesting that perhaps we should begin with the teachers at the level of their decision-making regarding the instructional program, and we are exploring new ways of working with teachers on a faculty so that their decisions will be rational and based on information.

We are building on the work of Guba, Trump, Miles, Brickell, and others in seeking new ways to utilize change agents in the school. The most promising idea to come out of the project so far is that of the developmental team as one way of moving a receptive faculty into responsible decision-making.

Little by little, we are learning how to change a school so that it can become not only more effective, but more receptive to change itself and more influential in helping others change. Slowly, and on a broken front, our country's most innovative schools are moving ahead, leading other more tradition-bound schools painfully into the 20th century.

Science Plus Innovative Educational Environment

David Krech

THOUGH THE BRAINS OF CHILDREN are bigger and better than those of rats, I find it difficult to believe that what we discover about rat-brain chemistry can deviate widely from what we will eventually discover about human-brain chemistry. This is, of course, a statement of belief and faith, not a statement of demonstrated fact. I believe, however, that what we in our laboratories are discovering in our rat brains today, you people in our schools will be applying to our grandchildren tomorrow.

TWO-STAGE MEMORY STORAGE PROCESS THEORY

To place animal research on the chemical mechanisms of memory and learning in their proper context, I will first review very briefly one of the major theories that guides this physiological research.

Eight, four, eight, eight, three, nine, nine. If I asked you now to repeat these numbers, most of you would be able to do so without difficulty, since seven digits is well within the immediate memory span of nonsenile adults. However, if I were to wait about 35 minutes before asking you to repeat these numbers, most of you would fail. For now I would not be testing your immediate memory but your long-term memory.

Of course, if you wished, you could with practice convert your short-term memory of those digits to a long-term one. For example, if you were to ask me to repeat these numbers — at any time — I could do so without hesitation, 848-8399 is my home telephone number, and these digits have long since gone from the short-term stage to the long-term stage.

You have now been introduced to the basic behavioral observations that lie behind the two-stage memory storage process theory. Let me now tell you something about one set of physiological speculations that have been made to account for short-term and long-term memories and the conversion of the one into the other.

According to these notions, immediately after every learning trial or, indeed after every experience, a short-lived, electro-chemical process is set up in the brain. This process is the physiological mechanism that carries the short-term memory. Within a few seconds or minutes, however, this process decays and disappears, but before doing so, if all systems are go, this short-term, electro-chemical process triggers off a second series of events in the brain. This second process is chemical in nature and involves, primarily, the production of new proteins and the induction of higher enzymatic activity levels in the brain cells. This second process is more enduring and serves as the physiological substrate of our long-term memory.

ELECTRICAL SHOCK AND THE MEMORY PROCESS

Now we are ready to take the two-stage memory storage process theory into the laboratory for testing, and the first laboratory we shall visit is that of Dr. Murray Jarvik of the Albert Einstein Medical School in New York.

According to everything I have said, it would follow that one approach to testing the theory would be to provide a subject with some experience or other, then interrupt the short-term, electro-chemical process immediately, that is before it has had an opportunity to establish the long-term process. If this were done, the subject should never develop a long-term memory for that experience.

The step-down procedure devised by Dr. Jarvik for experimenting with rats does just that. This procedure takes advantage of the fact that when a rat is placed on a small platform a few inches above the floor, it will step down onto that floor within a few seconds. The rat will do this consistently, day after day. Now suppose that on one day the floor is electrified and stepping onto it produces a painful foot-shock. When the rat is returned to the platform later — even 24 hours later — it will not budge from the platform but will remain there indefinitely. The rat thus has demonstrated that he has a long-term memory for that painful experience.

If we take another rat and interfere with his short-term memory process immediately after he has stepped onto the electrified floor, the rat should show no evidence of having experienced a shock when tested the next day. Why? We have not given his short-term, electro-chemical memory process an opportunity to initiate the long-term, protein-enzymatic process. To interrupt the short-term process, Jarvik passes a mild electric current across the brain of the animal. The current is not strong enough to cause irreparable harm to the brain cells, but it does result in a very high level of activation of the neurons all over the brain, thus disrupting the short-term, electrochemical memory process. If this treatment follows closely enough after the animal's first experience with the foot-shock and we test him, a day later, the rat does indeed act as if he had no memory of yesterday's event; he jauntily and promptly steps down from the platform with no apparent expectation of shock! When a long time interval is interposed between the first foot-shock and the electric current treatment, the rat does remember the foot-shock and remains on the platform when tested the next day. This again is what we should have expected from our theory. The short-term, electro-chemical process now has had time to set up the long-term, chemical memory process before it was disrupted.

Some well-known effects of accidental head injury in people seem to parallel these findings. Injuries that produce a temporary loss of consciousness, but no permanent damage to brain tissue, can cause the patient to experience a "gap" in his memory for the events just preceding the accident. This retrograde amnesia can be understood on the assumption that the events immediately prior to the accident were still being carried by the short-term memory processes at the time of the injury and their disruption by the injury was sufficient to prevent the induction of the long-term processes. The patient says "Where am I?" not only because he does not recognize the hospital but also because he cannot remember how he came to be injured.

SYNTHESIS OF NEW BRAIN PROTEINS AND THE MEMORY PROCESS

Let us now examine Dr. Bernard Agranoff's laboratory at the University of Michigan Medical School in Ann Arbor. Dr. Agranoff's work supports the hypothesis that the synthesis of new brain proteins is crucial for the establishment of the long-term memory process. He argues that if we can prevent the formation of new proteins in the brain, even though the short-term, electro-chemical memory process is not interfered with, the long-term memory process can never become established.

Much of Agranoff's work had been done with goldfish. The fish is placed in one end of a small rectangular tank, which is divided into two halves by a vertical barrier nearly reaching the water's surface. When a light is turned on, the fish must swim over the barrier into the other side of the tank within 20 seconds; otherwise, he receives an electric shock. This training is continued for several trials until the animal learns to swim rapidly to the other side as soon as the light is turned on. Most goldfish learn this shock-avoidance task quite easily and remember it over many days. Immediately before training — in some experiments immediately after — Agranoff injects the antibiotic puromycin into the goldfish's brain. Puromycin is a protein inhibitor that prevents the formation of new proteins in the brain's neurons. When injected, Agranoff finds that the goldfish are not impaired in their acquisition of the shock-avoidance task, but when tested a day or so later, they show almost no retention for the task.

These results are interpreted in two ways: The short-term memory process, which helps the animal remember from one trial to the next and thus permits him to learn in the first place, is not dependent upon the formation of new proteins. The long-term process, which can help the fish remember from one day to the next and would thus permit him to retain what he had learned, is dependent upon the production of new proteins. And again, just as in the instance of Jarvik's rats, if the puromycin injection comes more than an hour after learning, it has no effect on later memory because the long-term memory process presumably has already been set up and the inhibition of protein synthesis can now no longer affect memory. Here then, in this antibiotic, we have our first chemical memory erasure — or more accurately, a chemical, long-term memory preventative. Almost identical findings have been reported by other workers in other laboratories working with mice and rats, animals far removed from the goldfish.

CENTRAL-NERVOUS-SYSTEM STIMULANTS AND THE MEMORY PROCESS

James Lafayette McGaugh of the Psychology Department at San Jose State College, San Jose, California, argues that injections of central-nervous-system (CNS) stimulants like strychnine or picrotoxin or metrazol should enhance or fortify or extend the activity of the short-term, electro-chemical memory processes and thus increase the probability that they would be successful in initiating long-term memory processes. If this were so, then it would follow that the injection of CNS stimulants immediately before or after training would improve learning performance. And that is precisely what McGaugh and his mice sound — together with several additional results that have important implications.

In one of McGaugh's most revealing experiments, eight groups of mice from two quite different hereditary backgrounds and with hereditary differences in learning ability — a relatively bright strain and a relatively dull one — were given the problem of learning a fairly simple maze. Each of the four groups from each strain was injected with a different dosage of metrazol immediately after completing its learning trials. By properly dosing the animals with metrazol, the learning performance increased appreciably. Under the optimal dosage, the effect of the metrazol is so great that the dull mice, when treated with 10 mg/kg of body wt., do slightly better than their untreated, but hereditarily superior colleagues, the bright rats. Here we not only have a chemical facilitator of learning but one that acts as a great equalizer among hereditarily different groups.

If the dosage for the dull mice is increased from 0 to 5 to 10 mg/kg, their performance improves; but if the dosage is increased beyond the 10 mg point for the dull mice and beyond 5 mg/kg for the bright ones, the increased strength of the metrazol solution actually results in a deterioration in learning. Two inferences can be drawn from this last finding. First, the optimal dosage of chemical learning facilitators will vary greatly with the individual taking the drug (there is, in other words, an interaction between heredity and drugs), and second, there is a limit to the intellectual power of even a hopped-up Southern Californian super-mouse.

ENVIRONMENT AND THE CHEMISTRY AND ANATOMY OF THE BRAIN

It would seem clear, then, that we already have available a fairly extensive class of drugs that can facilitate learning and memory in animals. But a closer examination of McGaugh's results and the work of others also suggests that these drugs do not work in a monolithic manner on something called "learning" or "memory." In some instances the drugs seem to act on attentiveness; in some on the ability to vary one's attacks on a problem; in some on persistence; in some on immediate memory, in some on long-term memory. Different drugs work differentially for different strains, individuals, intellectual tasks, and learning components.

Do all of these results mean that we will soon be able to substitute a pharmacopoeia of drugs for our various school enrichment and innovative educational programs? Do they mean that most educators will soon be technologically unemployed or, if young enough, will have to turn in their schoolmaster's gown for a pharmacist's jacket? The answer is no, as our Berkeley laboratory experiments on the influence of education and training on brain anatomy and chemistry suggest.

This research, started some 15 years ago, was guided by the same general theory that has guided the more recent work, but our research strategy and tactics were quite different. Instead of interfering physiologically or chemically with animals to determine the effects of intervention upon memory storage — as did Jarvik, Agranoff, and McGaugh — we have taken the obverse question and, working only with normal animals, we had sought to determine the effects of memory storage on the chemistry and anatomy of the brain.

Our argument went as follows: If the establishment of long-term memory processes involves increased activity of brain enzymes, then animals that have been required to do a great deal of learning and remembering should terminate with brains enzymatically different from those of animals that have not been so challenged by their environment. This should be especially true for the enzymes involved in trans-synaptic neural activity. Further, since such neural activity would make demands on brain-cell action and metabolism, one might also expect to find various morphological differences between the brains of rats raised in psychologically stimulating environments and those raised in psychologically pallid environments.

In one standard experiment one rat from each of a dozen pairs of male twins is chosen by lot at weaning age to go into an educationally active and innovative environment — for rats, that is — while its twin brother is placed in as unstimulating an environment as we can contrive. All 12 educationally enriched pups live together in one large wire-mesh cage in a well-lighted, noisy, and busy laboratory. The cage is equipped with ladders, running wheels, and other "creative" rat "toys." For 30 minutes each day the rats are taken out of their cages and allowed to explore new territory. As the rats grow older, they are given various little learning tasks to master, for which they are rewarded with bits of sugar. This stimulating educational and training program is continued for 80 days.

While these animals are enjoying the richest intellectual environment Berkeley can provide for rats, each impoverished animal lives out his life in solitary confinement in a small cage situated in a dimly lit and quiet room. It is rarely handled by its keeper and never invited to explore new environments, to solve problems, or join in fun and games with fellow rats or graduate students. Both groups of rats, however, have unlimited access to the same standard food throughout the experiment. At the age of 105 days, as it must to all our experimental rats, enriched and impoverished alike, comes the day of reckoning. The rats are sacrificed, and their brains are dissected and analyzed morphologically and chemically.

This standard experiment, repeated dozens of times, has yielded the following results. As the fortunate littermate lives out his life in the educationally enriched condition, the bulk of his cortex expands and grows deeper and heavier than that of his culturally deprived brother. Part of this increase in cortial mass is accounted for by an increase in the number of glia cells — specialized brain cells that play vital functions in the nutrition of the neurons and perhaps also in laying down permanent memory traces — part of it by an increase in the size of the neuronal cell bodies and their nuclei, and part by an increase in the diameters of the blood vessels supplying the cortex. Our postulated chemical changes also occur. The enriched brain shows more acetylcholinesterase, the enzyme involved in the trans-synaptic conduction of neural impulses, and cholinesterase, the enzyme found primarily in the glia cells.

Finally, in another series of experiments, we demonstrated that these structural and chemical changes are the signs of a "good" brain. That is, we have shown that either via early rat-type Headstart programs or via selective breeding programs, we can increase the weight and density of the rat's cortex and its acetylcholinesterase and cholinesterase activity levels. And when we do so — by either method — we find that we have created superior problem-solving animals.

This means that the effects of the psychological and educational environment are not restricted to something called the "mental" realm. On the other hand, permitting a young rat to grow up in an educationally and experientially inadequate and unstimulating environment creates an animal with a relatively deteriorated brain — a brain with a thin and light cortex, lowered blood supply, diminished enzymatic activities, smaller neuronal cell bodies, and fewer glia cells. A lack of adequate educational fare for the young animal — no matter how adequate the food supply or how good the family — and a lack of adequate psychological enrichment results in palpable, measurable deteriorative changes in the brain's chemistry and anatomy.

Let us now return to McGaugh's results for a moment. Whether and to what extent this or that drug will improve the animal's learning ability will depend, of course, on what the drug does to the rat's brain chemistry. What it does to the rat's brain chemistry will depend upon the status of the chemistry in the brain to begin with, and what the status of the brain's chemistry is to begin with, as demonstrated by the

Berkeley experiments, reflects the rat's early psychological and educational environment. Therefore, whether and to what extent any drug will improve an animal's attention, or memory, or learning ability will depend upon the animal's past experiences. I am not talking — to repeat again — about some kind of interaction between mental factors on the one hand and chemical compounds on the other. I am talking about interactions between chemical factors introduced into the brain by the biochemist's injection or pills and chemical factors induced in the brain by the educator's stimulating or impoverishing environment. It is as straightforward and as wondrous as that. The biochemist's work can be only half effective without the educator's help.

IMPLICATIONS FOR EDUCATORS

What kind of educational environment can best develop the brain — chemically and morphologically? What kind of stimulation makes for an enriched environment? What educational experiences can potentiate the effects of the biochemist's drugs? We don't know. The biochemist doesn't know. It is at this point that I see a whole new area of collaboration in basic research between the educator, the psychologist, and the neurobiochemist. What I am referring to is, essentially, a research program that combines the Agranoff and McGaugh technique with our Berkeley approach. Given the start that has already been made in the animal laboratory, an intensive program of research — with animals and with children — that seeks to spell out the interrelations between chemical and educational influences on brain and memory can have tremendous results. And this need not wait for the future. We know enough now to start. I have not forgotten that all my data thus far come from the brains of goldfish and rodents. But, can the educator be certain that the chemistry of the brain of a rat — which, after all, is a fairly complex mammal — is so different from that of the brain of a human being? Can he, therefore, dare neglect this challenge — or even gamble — when the stakes are so high?

There is another role in all this for the educator of the future. This will be a role in applied education, but here again he will have to collaborate with the biochemist. Both the biochemist and the teacher of the future will combine their skills and insights for the educational and intellectual development of the child. Richard needs a bit more of an immediate-memory stimulator; Martha could probably do with a chemical attention-span stretcher; Rachel needs an anti-cholinesterase to slow down her mental processes a bit; Joan, some puromycin — she remembers too many details and gets lost.

Improbable as this may sound, I mean all of it quite literally. Educators know much already about the innovative hardware of education — computer-assisted instruction, 8mm cartridge loading projectors, micro-transparencies, and so on. Now educators must consider the software, or rather the "chemware," of education — enzyme-assisted instruction, protein memory consolidators, antibiotic memory repellers, and so forth — for these are the kinds of things educators will be vitally concerned with in the year 2000. The time to initiate this concern is now.

State of Technology in Education and Its Further Development and Implementation

Overviews

THE GRAND SPECTRUM OF
EDUCATIONAL TECHNOLOGY

Dwight Allen

Though educational technology promises to have a major impact on education, its use must be viewed as part of the total educational picture, which includes not only materials and machines but people. In this perspective, the whole learning system can be labeled a nonhardware technology. By examining this system as a technology, experimental techniques then can be used to develop better methods of practice teaching, to differentiate meaningfully the roles of the teaching staff, and to overcome the problems of the group process, the very essence of education.

In considering the mechanics of education, technology can be seen as changing the rules. It is affecting the structure and availability of knowledge through the use of data banks, random-access devices, programed learning, computer-assisted instruction, and disposable materials. It is also broadening the scope and making the use of educational materials more efficient through the low cost and ease of duplication. The learning environment also is changing because of technological advances — a new standard of constancy has been developed, and different levels of flexibility now can be achieved.

Technology itself is constantly changing and must be constantly improved. Educators can stimulate such improvement through imaginative use, for use yields multiplication effects; technological advances form new technologies and effective combinations.

COMPUTER-BASED INSTRUCTION SYSTEMS

Allen B. Corderman

A computer-based instructional system provides the only serious hope of accommodating individual differences in mass education. Essentially, this system involves a method by which an individual student can receive and respond to information presented from a gigantic storage bank.

There are three modes of computer presentation: the drill-and-practice mode, in which the student exercises a skill to which he previously has been exposed; the tutorial mode, in which the computer presents information to the student and then tests him on retention and understanding; and the dialogue mode, in which the student imparts information and instructions to the computer.

Using such computer methodology, the teacher will be free to plan course presentations in smaller units of time with selected groups of students, acting as a tutor to small groups of relatively homogeneous children.

The computer can aid the teacher, as well as the counselor and the school administrator, in other ways. It can correct responses, maintain records, and develop and grade tests or homework materials. In addition, teaching and testing methods can be standardized through the development of computer routines compatible with the student's learning process.

TECHNOLOGY: THE MEDIUM, NOT THE MESSAGE

Leonard A. Muller

Students may have a favorite teacher; they will never have a favorite computer. The style of education a machine makes possible is entirely dependent upon the needs, imagination, goals, and, above all, the social and human values of the educators who use these tools. The things a computer can do constitute a great gift — the gift of time — time to think, to imagine, to explore ideas, to evaluate efforts and values, to be creative.

However, educators must recognize the limitations of machines if the use of technology is to stimulate an academic boom rather than an academic depression. The computer cannot handle values or qualities, affections or attitudes. It cannot inspire a student to greatness, nor can it substitute for the personal relations between student and teacher. Moreover, the computer's performance can never be any better than the programed information fed into it.

The dangers of over-control in the use of technology by business and government must also be considered. The greatest deterrent against over-control is the early, positive participation by educators in the use of emerging technologies.

HUMANISTIC TECHNOLOGY

John Henry Martin

Excessive reliance on too narrow a base of learning theory and use of engineering terms like "terminals" and "multi-media" are hampering computer-assisted instruction. The main concern should be with the educational behavior of computers, which must approximate that of human beings in a tutorial relationship with one another. Computers should not be mere page-turners, utilizing only the visual sense of the learner, but should enable the learner to use as many senses as possible. To stimulate the development of such instruments, educators must inform manufacturers of their needs and assist in designing appropriate programing for the new hardware.

In teaching reading, for example, programing produced for the talking typewriter has enabled five-year-olds to attain in four months a greater reading level and comprehension than that attained by six-year-olds in a school year. Of equal importance is the fact that this instrument has been instituted within the framework of the total educational system, with the teacher and the community as vital parts of the process.

TECHNOLOGICAL TOOLS: FLEXIBLE AND EFFICIENT
Richard H. Bell

Educators should not wait for the perfection of technology or for the so-called revolution in education; technology can be used efficiently right now. If we were to "invent" education today, we would find it inconceivable not to use the many advantages offered by modern technology. Educators have the responsibility and the means to determine whether technological aids will become effective tools or mere fads.

Television is an especially effective educational tool. It can structure reality into learning experiences for many viewers in many different locations and often affords better visibility than if the viewer were actually present at an event. Moreover, television is a device for individualizing instruction since it can store information that may be retrieved by the learner when he needs it. The different television configurations available for a variety of educational needs also make it economically feasible.

Efficient use of television, and modern technology in general, will be determined by the educators who must control and use these tools to improve the quality of education.

THE POTENTIAL EDUCATIONAL IMPACT OF TELEVISION

John B. Burns

Compared with the growth and success of commerical television, educational television has stagnated. More money will not provide a cure for ETV. Instead, the particular power of commercial television must be analyzed to see what lessons can be applied. Commerical television is not mere entertainment or escapism; it presents the viewer with life situations. Weekly dramatic programs, for example, under the umbrella of entertainment, deal with human relationships, spheres and aspects of responsibility, and areas of initiative and judgment. In these areas, television can serve formal education by presenting what is not being taught in the classroom or by supporting what is being taught. It should not be used to teach what is being taught in the classroom, as it is used now in the form of teachers lecturing on the screen.

If educators know what they want to present in the supportive areas of education, television can be utilized effectively through its structure of entertainment. For example, in planning reading programs, educators might look to programs on commercial television such as the game shows and cartoon shows, which present songs with words and a bouncing ball. Both types of shows stimulate reading and word comprehension in an entertaining fashion. Using television to do what it does best — entertain — can result in a valuable expansion and enrichment of education.

The Grand Spectrum of Educational Technology

Dwight Allen

NEW EDUCATIONAL TECHNOLOGY promises to have a major impact on educational materials, the organizational system of the school, the learning environment, and the structure and availability of knowledge. The use of educational technology, however, is not a simplistic thing. There are a wide range of variables that could affect both the use of technology in education and the adaptation of education to our technological age. In viewing the place of technology in the total educational picture, the concern here is with the image, with the grand spectrum of something called educational technology, rather than with details.

Before viewing this grand spectrum, we should consider some peripheral issues that are vital to any consideration of educational technology because they are vital to education in general. First is the issue of image-making in education. Our image in education is worse than the former image of the prune; if people were asked to associate something with a prune, they always thought of a dark, dirty, wrinkled laxative. Prune sales increased incredibly when advertising began to show prunes against white beds of cottage cheese and pictured prominent people running down the road saying, "We like prunes." Educators too need to think about their image and the image of education in general.

George Gallop put this very succinctly at a conference several years ago. He said that when he conducted surveys for the motion picture industry to determine whether a film should be made, the final question was always, "Do you think this film will have educational value?" If the answer was "Yes," his advice was not to produce the film because nobody would pay to see a film that had educational value.

Image-making is thus one great problem educators face today. Another problem is that of lures. We should utilize the profit motivation for educational improvement. Education is a huge business. There is money to be made in education, and there are careers to be made. Why apologize for these things? Why not use them? We like it when IBM designs something useful for us, but we are not sure whether they should make money as a result.

More specific to the central consideration of educational technology is the issue of noneducational technology. Educational technology must be coordinated with noneducational technology because the latter has educational implications. For example, the fact that our population is becoming more mobile has an educational implication. Mobility has been achieved through noneducational technology, but it will influence greatly educational decision-making. We, however, have not started to interact at that level yet.

EDUCATIONAL MATERIALS

These peripheral issues must be kept in mind as we explore the facets of educational technology. One facet of this spectrum is educational materials, and here educational technology is changing the rules. One of these changes results from the present availability, ease, and low cost of duplication. The ditto machine no longer reigns supreme; xerography and other new methods are now making the widespread reproduction of masters possible. This fact has a profound implication for the use of materials. For example, teachers formerly did not keep things because they had only one copy; this rule does not apply anymore.

Moreover materials are more accessible now. For example, United Airlines has the blueprint specifications for the Boeing-707 on microfiche in a little cabinet. If an engineer wants a blow-up of a part of the wing structure, he orders it, is given a copy, uses it, and throws it away. Industry has found that it is cheaper to make the engineer a copy that he can then throw away than to retrieve and refile it an original. This type of accessibility is possible in the schools too.

Educational technology is also affecting the variety, combination, and systems of materials, and it is affecting the production of materials — external, teacher, and student. For example, student-produced materials are becoming increasingly important. Anyone who is associated in any way with a faculty should see the student-produced film called *The Idaho Test*. A spoof on standardized tests, it is one of the best statements of what dangers lie in standardized tests. Technology, in terms of routine student productions within the context of an individual class, is becoming usual. The era of the written report as the major vehicle of communication is over, but we haven't discovered that in school yet. We object to the fact that children don't read at home, that instead they will watch a National Geographic production on Leakey's expedition in Africa, for example; but watching such educational programs is as good an education as can be found anywhere. I will never forget my own English teacher who, when she found out that *Macbeth* was being produced in San Francisco, changed our assignment to *The Merchant of Venice* because she was afraid we would go see the play and not have to read it.

And there is the issue of the revision of educational materials. The constant problem of outdating is going to become worse. In education we are almost at the point where we can't afford to wait for textbooks to be produced because materials are changing so rapidly. Right now a textbook production schedule is usually about a five-year process from package to plate, and we can't afford that time lapse any more. Therefore, we need to think about alternatives as well as the timing of revisions.

One of the most delightful results of such thinking is the use of something for purposes for which it was never intended. Bob Mager wrote a handbook on preparing instructional objectives for programers. Programers may use it, but virtually everybody else in the country is also using it as a way of defining performance criteria. Why fight it? Does the fact that it is used for purposes for which it wasn't designed make it less good? I think not. We have to be alert to alternatives in the use of materials.

We must also increase alternatives in the organizational processes of the school. Here technology can be very useful, for it can furnish the educator with alternative ways of performing routine, mechanical tasks now done by the teacher. For example, attendance taking can be simplified through a system we call SCRAM, Stanford Comprehensive Randomized Attendance Monitoring. We find that more accurate attendance can be taken in a typical school by consulting a table of random numbers every period; attendance is taken in two or three classes and generalized over a period of time. If you want to prove the accuracy of this system, all you have to do is scoop up about 40 students in the hall, hold them until attendance is taken, and then let them go back to their classes. You will find that about 12 out of the 40 were not marked absent. The 100 per cent attendance-accounting procedure is very inaccurate the way it is now done. Moreover, teachers hate it, for it involves a professional in an inappropriate, mechanical task.

The other part of the SCRAM attendance-accounting procedure that is interesting is the development of what is called a "hot list." It is true that about 2 per cent of the students in a school are responsible for 70 per cent of the absences, and we are now keeping track of the 98 per cent for whom it doesn't make any difference. The SCRAM method puts those 2 per cent on a hot list that is then circulated. It is surprising how hard students work to keep off that list.

Easier communications are also essential in the educational organization. As educational systems become more complex, with teams of teachers working with each other and interaction between teachers and materials, the process of communication becomes completely overpowering. Somehow we have to cut through that.

Finally, there is the issue of organizing student data, for example, grouping variables. We have used ability; now we are starting to use interest in such groupings. We are also beginning to identify new variables, such as assignment variables, but we don't have the whole process of student data organized very well yet.

LEARNING ENVIRONMENT

Generally then, educational technology is being used and will be used to broaden and make more effective the use of educational materials and equipment. Another facet of education that is being improved greatly through technology is the learning environment. We now can develop a new standard of constancy in the environment. For example, we can manipulate the temperature, the lighting, and many more elements of the environment.

And we have different levels of flexibility. Flexibility is no longer an either-or proposition — either I can move it or I can't. The questions that should be asked now are, "What level of flexibility and what special relationships do we need?"

We used to have the image of one teacher attached to one classroom. This is not a good image. For one thing, it is wasteful. Contemplating 30 empty chairs during a preparation period is not a very efficient method of operation. Furthermore, if we are going to have small-group instruction, we need an environment that is good for small groups. If we want large-group instruction, we need a different kind of area.

The aesthetics of this learning environment also need to be examined. Today any time a budget is tightened, the first things eliminated are the aesthetic aspects of the environment. We spend hundreds of thousands of dollars trying to motivate students, yet one of the simplest ways to motivate students is to put them in a pleasant environment. Is that so profound? Is it so unusual? Does it violate intuition? No, but look at the instructional sterility of the school. It is not a warm, soft, interesting place to be. We need to make schools warm, soft, interesting places to be. For example, most of the studies show that you can put a carpet in a school and maintain it over a 20-year period for less than the cost of asphalt tile in terms of the initial cost and its maintenance. There isn't a reason in the world why carpets shouldn't be on every school floor. It is a puritanical notion that carpeting is a frill and we can't afford frills.

We also need multiple definitions of separation. Small groups do not always need to be acoustically separate. There are other ways to accomplish separation — audio-separation, acclimated separation, visual separation, physical separation, or new applications of existing alternatives such as background music and different uses of lighting.

STRUCTURE AND AVAILABILITY OF KNOWLEDGE

When we consider the learning environment, we must also consider the structure and availability of knowledge. Here too, educational technology can play an important role. Data banks, random-access devices, programed learning, computer-assisted instruction, and disposable materials should be considered. Since we have disposable dresses, why can't we have disposable materials? It is our puritanical heritage that makes us want to keep track of everything. Some librarians, for example, are happiest when materials are in and students are out.

Data banks, computer-assisted instruction, and so on, demand sophistication at the content level. For example, when we become expert in the use of data banks, selection of information will be a problem. At present if a student goes into a library and requests materials on the Suez Canal, the librarian dumps 7,000 items on the Suez Canal in his lap. We are going to have to become a little more sophisticated. We are going to have to be able to tell the machine that we want enough but not too much. And we are going to have to be able to tell the machine now to define "enough." Sophistication, then, is going to be a real issue when we get data banks, random-access devices, and disposable materials in the process of education.

The development of new standards of classification must also be considered. We organize everything into categories, and that is silly. In the United States, science is in one department and math is in another; in South America, biology and chemistry are in one department and physics and mathematics in another. If you consider the latter a silly way to organize things, why is it that in American schools typing is taught in the business department and handwriting is taught in the English department? The reason for this inanity is that by historical accident secretaries were the first ones to use typewriters. There is no conceptual reason why typewriting shouldn't be taught in the English department. There are too many of these anachronisms in education.

Putting computer-assisted instruction into operation also presents difficulties. We presently have to advance to the tune of the computer. At Stanford we are working on a unit of computer-assisted instruction in teacher education, and we have found that each individual favors a different kind of response from the computer in return for a correct answer. Our computer sometimes responds "good," sometimes "excellent," and sometimes it says "wow." Some people giggled and liked "wow," and other people thought it was frivolous. Consequently, one of the things we are going to do is individualize computer-assisted instruction just for fun. This might not mean anything, but it at least demonstrates what can be done with a little imagination.

In structuring knowledge, imagination should also be utilized to explore the entertainment potential of education. Seeking to make education entertaining is not a new concept. During World War II, for example, Walt Disney made films in which Donald Duck showed how to repair a piston. These films were tremendously entertaining, and people who were not even interested in repairing pistons liked to look at them. Today this entertainment potential has been enhanced greatly through new developments in technology that make a more sophisticated achievement of this aim as possible as it is desirable.

Other aspects of the structure and availability of knowledge that must also be considered by today's educators are the great availability of information and the general sophistication of students, the latter being partially a consequence of the former. Students are much more sophisticated now than they used to be, and they are much less willing to believe in the infallibility of teachers. Yet the system, as designed, assumes that infallibility.

IMPROVEMENT OF TECHNOLOGY

Technology, then, can be used in structuring knowledge, in improving the learning environment, and in broadening the scope of educational materials. But technology itself is not a static thing. It must be constantly improved, and educators should serve to stimulate such improvement. Initially, when technology is used, it becomes a leverage to encourage the use of more technology, which, in turn, becomes a leverage for improvement.

When an educator first considers a technological innovation, there are problems of laboratory improvement versus field testing, versus trial implementation, and sometimes educators need to leap-frog over all of this and try something on a broad scale immediately. Educators have to decide when to employ the long process and when to short-circuit it.

Use will yield multiplication effects; technological advances form new technologies. Use will also yield effective combinations. One technology taken by itself may fail; three or four put together may succeed. Computer-assisted instruction by itself is not very good, but together with other things, it can be an excellent aid to teaching. Therefore, we must design teacher educational programs that train teachers to anticipate new technologies and teach them new uses of existing technology, such as computer diagnostics.

NONHARDWARE TECHNOLOGY

The technology we have been considering can be called hardware technology; we also must orientate ourselves to non-hardware technology — the idea of learning systems, which have never been thought of as a technology before.

Look, for example, at the educational concept of "remedial." In Webster's dictionary "remedial" is defined as "something you get over." In education, remedial is not something you get over. How many people ever got over being remedial in arithmetic or being remedial in English? Remedial in education means we have given up. Perhaps only the injection of massive amounts of resources into the early primary grades or pre-school will remedy the situation. Maybe we should spend five thousand dollars a year on the education of each preprimer. The idea frightens me, however, because I am not sure if we had five thousand dollars a year for each child that we would know how to spend it. Thus, we need to examine learning systems in entirely new terms — as a technology.

One aspect of new learning systems is the idea of micro-teaching as a technique in teacher education. This is a new kind of practice in which teachers begin by working with classes of four or five that are constructed for their benefit. They are really teaching. The children are real children, and they are learning real things, but the classes are held at the teachers' convenience. Moreover, the lessons are short — four or five minutes. All these new practices may develop teachers who have original ideas on the techniques of teaching and learning. Thus, this experiment can be considered a technological one.

The problems of group process can also be considered as part of the technology of learning systems. We are just learning to view group process in this light. At present, for example, there are too many rituals in group process. That we need to be open is the catch-word of the typical group. This means when one is in a group, he follows the ritual by saying just enough so that everybody thinks he is open. We must eliminate such restrictive rituals.

Learner-monitor teaching is another aspect of group-process technology. Bob Mager found, for example, that he could take a two-and-a-half week training course and compress it into three hours by letting the learner determine what he wanted to know about a particular subject.

Finally, we need a differentiated staff in our learning system. We need to have different people paid different amounts to do different things. What should an eighteen thousand dollars-a-year teacher do that a five-thousand dollars-a-year teacher does not do? Today the only way a teacher advances is to grow older on the job or to take more units. These are the worst possible criteria for advancing teachers. The reason we do not have any other criteria is that we really do not know the differences there should be in basic teacher roles. All teachers do the same thing from the day they arrive in the teaching profession until the day they retire. We can't afford that. Our whole learning system cannot afford that.

Thus, technology should be applied to our very system of learning just as it should be applied to the structure and availability of knowledge, the learning environment, and the use of educational materials. Through the utilization and improvement of technology in these vast areas, education can indeed be changed for the better. The spectrum is vast and the possibilities infinite.

Computer-Based
Instruction Systems

Allen B. Corderman

ALTHOUGH DATA-PROCESSING equipment has been installed and utilized in school systems throughout the country for several years now, it is actually only in the recent past that people have given serious thought to how we could use such a system for supplementing or improving the educational process itself. Data-processing systems are ideal tools for performing some of the repetitive functions associated with school administration, thereby relieving the school administrator and his staff for more significant efforts. We can make use of the data-processing system to relieve the teacher from rote-type duties and, at the same time, contribute significantly to his teaching methods and his information about his students' progress.

To bring a certain historical perspective to this consideration of the effects of the computer on education, we might go back to a typical grammar school in the Middle Ages. Let us ask ourselves, "What was the process of teaching like before books were introduced into the educational system?" It is quite plausible to draw a number of parallels between the introduction of books and the coming introduction of computers as instructional devices.

In the 14th century, for example, a grammar school in England had an instructional program something like the following. On most days the teacher would read selected portions of a text from a manuscript and would explain parts of that text as he went along, usually repeating each sentence twice. Students were expected to memorize what the teacher said. On the following day, classwork would begin with a recitation — by the class as a whole or by individual students — of what had been covered on the previous day. There were no printed books, of course, and even the manuscripts available for use by the teachers were very rare. The process of education was almost entirely oral, with only a very limited use of visual materials of any sort.

Comparing that situation with what occurs today, we are immediately struck by the extent to which printed materials dominate school instruction. Although the place of books in our society is now widespread, it should be remembered that the printing of books on a large scale did not really occur until the 18th century.

There is every reason to think that a revolution in the educational system comparable to that occasioned by the introduction of textbooks has already begun with the use of computer-based devices as instructional aids. The most conservative forecast of developments during the next one hundred years in education must assign a prominent place to computers and their devices in any predicted configuration of future classrooms.

A FUTURE COMPUTER-BASED SYSTEM

What might a typical computer-based system look like over the next decade? In the first place, as the name implies, a computer itself is a part of a system. Computers come in all sizes and shapes, but there is basically a direct relationship between the size of the computer and how much work it can do. For example, a computer system that might be adequate for offering instructional materials to approximately 200 students at one time would fill a room of approximately 1,000 square feet or an average of two large-sized living rooms. Included in such a complex would be a series of large magnetic tape machines, capable of storing massive amounts of information and comparable in size to a well-stocked school library. In addition there would be devices capable of searching out particular information from a particular tape and either transforming that information or delivering it to another location as required. Other devices are available by which various people can add information to the memory system, can review information contained therein, or can change the content of the information presently in storage.

Finally, there would be devices for transmitting appropriate information to and from the computer system, which represent the link between the computer itself and other devices that might be thousands of miles away. However, for the teacher and the student to take advantage of this system, there must be some device located in proximity to the classroom by which teachers and students can communicate with the computer. These are called instructional terminals, and they consist of a device by which information is presented to the user and a device by which the user can respond to the information.

Thus, a computer-based instructional system essentially involves a method by which an individual student can receive information from a gigantic storage bank of information and can respond to the information so presented.

It is one thing to recognize that the computer technology developed to date makes it possible to introduce computer systems into the educational process. It is quite another thing, however, to explain why such technology should be introduced in the first place and to determine its advantages and limitations for education. We should, therefore, consider some of the characteristics of computer-based instruction that represent *advantages* to the educational process.

Individual Differences

One advantage stems from the well-known and most important psychological generalization that definite and clearly significant individual differences exist among children of a given group or class. We have all known for many years that children enter school with remarkably different abilities and that they will work at different rates and at different levels of accuracy and understanding. Nevertheless, for obvious economic reasons, we are not able to offer a curriculum program to each child according to his needs. We simply cannot afford that many teachers.

And yet, with each passing year, the ratio between teachers and students becomes increasingly more critical. For example, where ten years ago there were approximately twenty-five children in a classroom, there are now, on the average, thirty-two. As this number increases, the possibilities of individual attention to each student will grow increasingly more remote. It would appear, therefore, that if things continue as they are, we will violate the principle of individual differences and its effects on education even more severely in the future than we have in the past.

If, on the other hand, we can introduce into the educational process a system that supplements classroom instruction and is sensitive to individual differences, we can essentially "have our cake and eat it, too." We need something with which we can individualize the presentation of the curriculum to each and every child, and this something can be a computer-based instructional system. The best single reason for using computers for instruction is that computer technology provides the only serious hope for recognition of individual differences in subject matter learning.

Elimination of Routine Chores

Another important task for the computer is to eliminate routine chores for the teacher, the counselor, and the school administrator. These include, as a minimum, correcting responses, keeping records, and developing and grading tests, quizzes, or homework materials.

Children can be quizzed by a computer on the subject matter exposed to them by the teacher, and appropriate records of each child's performance can be stored and recalled at the teacher's request. In addition, the massive capacity of the computer system for storing information regarding students' performances make available the data appropriate for performing educational research and analyzing the effects of innovative techniques, methodologies, and curricula material on the learning process.

Standardization of Course Content and Testing

Another process that is particularly well suited to computer-based instruction is the standardization of both teaching and testing methods by virtue of the curriculum materials available from the computer for the student. As we study in detail how children learn and perform, we can develop computer routines that are compatible with the student's learning process. For example, the routine introduction and practice of standard skills such as arithmetic can be handled by computer-based terminals. The teacher can then move to the much more challenging and important task of trouble shooting. He or she can help those children who are unsuccessful with the material we are giving to the majority of the children. Although we can expect to become more familiar with the learning process and the types of materials most appropriate to that process in the future, it is inevitable in these early years that the depth of programing and the number of alternatives we can offer will be insufficient to accommodate all children.

Furthermore, as we experiment with curriculum materials and methods of presenting them to children, we can expect to evolve gradually a standard teaching and testing process that is consistent with the learning process itself. This will largely eliminate the problem we frequently encounter in which different schools offer the same material at different points in a child's educational experience. An ultimate goal, therefore, would be to standardize the order of presentation and the teaching or testing techniques, particularly for the elementary and high school systems, in such a fashion that an individual child can move from one school to another or from one classroom to another, and be quickly located among his educational peers.

This approach, however, is in no sense intended to imply that the individual flavor of a particular teacher and his unique methods of imparting information to his class will be lost to a regimented and arbitrary method of teaching. Rather it suggests that techniques will become available by which each teacher can quickly determine the achievement levels of each student in the class and evaluate these against common criteria of achievement.

MODES OF PRESENTATION

There are various modes by which computer-based instructional materials can be presented to the student. Although various authors may use different names to describe the same phenomena, there are basically three modes of instruction that can be identified at this time: drill and practice, tutorial, and dialogue.

Before examining these modes of instruction, we should consider certain general characteristics of computer-based instruction.

The computer system can be located any distance from the

student terminals, and the information can be transmitted over a telephone line. Thus, for example, one computer located in some central headquarters within a city can serve students located in several different schools or several different classrooms within a given school.

The student terminal is essentially a teletype machine by which the material is presented on paper and on which the student types his responses. Such a system serves two purposes: (1) the student tears off his personal copy at the end of the lesson and, therefore, has a record of his own performance, and (2) the terminal transmits all answers by the student back to the computer for later reference by the teacher.

By keeping track of the student's performance, the computer thus has a record of each student's progress, and the next lesson can be planned, based upon a child's achievements to date. This is the heart of the individualized-instructional concept.

The actual scoring technique is determined by the curriculum developer, who is the person responsible for preparing the course material, determining the order of presentation, and planning the method of scoring. It is important to note, however, that any one of these characteristics can be altered to suit an individual teacher's requirements. This is accomplished by "instructing" the computer to change the procedure from that which it is presently using.

At the end of each day's session on the terminal, a student is shown how many errors he made and on what problems, the number of time-outs and what problems, and a history of errors and time for the total concept block to date. In addition to this information, the teacher can request up to 100 different types of information from the computer pertaining to individual students or different groups of students.

One of the most widespread criticisms of a computer-based instructional system has been that it will take the place of the teacher in the educational system and that, indeed, in the future teachers may no longer be necessary at all. Such is not the case. On the contrary, the teacher's role is as important in a computer-based instructional system as it ever has been. The computer is only a supplement to the teaching situation and not a substitute, and the teacher continues to impart the educational information to the student and to develop the concepts that, in the aggregate, represent an education.

Drill and Practice

How, then, does the first mode of presentation, drill and practice, supplement the work of the teacher? What does the term "drill and practice" mean?

Drill and practice is exercising a skill to which the student has been previously exposed in the classroom situation. This is the everyday experience associated with practicing — via homework, workbooks, quizzes, and so forth — material described by the teacher. It is the drill-and-practice mode that we can handle most easily and effectively, particularly as it is applied to the various skill subjects such as reading, mathematics, and foreign languages. In a typical situation, a student will be exposed in the classroom to a concept associated, for example, with mathematics. He can then practice his ability to utilize that concept at an instructional terminal and can be immediately aware of his skill level by virtue of his performance at the terminal. The teacher, furthermore, can determine how well the skill has been learned by evaluating the student's performance in the drill-and-practice mode.

For example, Stanford University in Palo Alto, California, is presenting drill-and-practice material in elementary school mathematics to approximately 900 children daily. The material is broken up into weekly concept blocks, and the order of presenting each block can be varied according to the individual teacher's wishes or requirements.

The student's activities relative to the drill-and-practice

mode are as follows. On each concept block the child begins with a pre-test. On the basis of his pre-test score, he is placed in one of five levels for five days of training. He moves up and down in these five levels, depending upon his score on each day. If, for example, he makes a score between 60 and 79 per cent inclusive, he remains at the same level. If he makes 80 per cent or higher, he is branched upward one level, and if he makes below 60 per cent he is branched downward. At the end of the five days of training, each student is then given a post-test, which is entered into his record for that particular concept block.

At the same time that he is working on a particular concept block, he is also being individually reviewed on earlier concepts on which his work was the least satisfactory as determined by his previous post-test scores. In the Stanford system, this review work consists of approximately 30 per cent of the day's work at the terminal.

Individualization in this drill-and-practice material is therefore occurring in two ways. The first way is to adjust the difficulty level of the exercise according to student performance. This adjustment is reflected in the five difficulty levels and the ability to move among them. The second way is to review individually each student on those past concepts in which his progress has been the weakest and, therefore, on which he needs more practice.

Tutorial

The next higher mode of instruction is the tutorial. In the tutorial mode, the computer is programed to present information to the student and then test the student on his retention and understanding of the information. For instance, the tutorial mode can be employed to teach reading comprehension in an elementary school situation. The student is presented with a paragraph and is then tested on his comprehension of the material it contained. Each paragraph has been previously evaluated for its level of difficulty. As in the drill-and-practice mode, each student can move up and down through various levels of difficulty, depending upon his individual performance.

One characteristic of the tutorial mode that is quite different from the drill-and-practice mode is that a student can be exposed to a system of branching in which the information content presented will vary as a function of the student's achievement. If, for example, a particular child consistently makes errors when exposed to a particular block of material, the computer can recognize the existence of a problem and introduce to the student additional descriptive information that will aid him in understanding and correcting his mistakes.

The tutorial method of teaching is presently being applied in the Brentwood School in a suburb of Palo Alto. Children in the first grade are being exposed to elementary arithmetic and spelling, using the tutorial system. Based upon teachers' interviews and children's enthusiasm for the system and the course, it would appear that a significant improvement in the educational process can be expected.

Dialogue

The ultimate mode for computer-based instruction is variously called dialogue, modeling, or simulation. In this mode, the computer not only imparts information to the student and evaluates the student's response, but the student himself can impart information or instructions to the computer. For example, if a student is taking a course in advanced mathematics, he may not want to perform the necessary arithmetic to solve a problem. He can then inform the computer of what the equation is and the appropriate parameters and coefficients of the equation and ask the computer to do the arithmetic for him. The student has demonstrated his knowledge by selecting the appropriate equation and the parameters therein, and the assumption is made that he already is knowledgeable about the arithmetical process. This mode of operation has not been utilized in an elementary classroom situation, primarily because it requires a heavy utilization of the computer and, therefore, significantly restricts the number of children who can perform the dialogue mode simultaneously. It has, however, been widely used in advanced education and in the military environment where it often goes under the title of "gaming."

EDUCATIONAL EFFECTS OF COMPUTERS

Finally, let us now look several years into the future and try to predict what the effects of a computer-based instructional system will be on a school system. What changes will occur in the educational process itself and to the people responsible for educating our children? In the first place, we can predict, with a rather high degree of confidence, that the types of materials to be employed in a computer-based context will greatly expand over the few skill subjects presently programed. In particular, mathematics, language arts, foreign languages, physical and biological sciences, and a large variety of vocational courses will be programed.

In addition, we can anticipate that the course levels will extend from at least the first grade through the college graduate levels. Publishers, who have rightly assumed that their product consisted of the printed page, will broaden their capabilities and products. They will be working directly with electronic corporations to prepare educational materials in computer language appropriate for utilization by schools with instructional terminals.

The teacher will become trained to review the instructional

materials stored in the computer and to edit or modify that information to satisfy his own teaching methods. The student will be so familiar with the instructional terminal that he or she will be unable to appreciate the fact that some schools don't have such things. We have found this consistently true in the Palo Alto area, where the children have worked on instructional terminals since the first grade.

By taking advantage of the individualized instruction and the individual knowledge of abilities, teachers will be able to plan their course presentation in terms of small units of time and small selected groups of students. The 50-minute hour traditionally used in schools will disappear, and, instead, each teacher will block out various periods of time ranging, for example, from 10 or 15 minutes to an hour or more or whatever he feels is necessary to impart a certain block of information. This planning can be conducted on a day-by-day basis and varied, depending upon the level of achievement accomplished.

Furthermore, the teacher's role will become that of an instructor or tutor to small groups of relatively homogeneous children. In this sense he will impart conceptual information to his group and then troubleshoot on an individual basis whenever problems are identified. This is a much more challenging opportunity for the teacher than lecturing and demonstrating to large groups of children as he does today. Although his responsibilities will be no less significant, they will now be channeled much more strongly toward the individual child's capabilities and needs.

A typical day, therefore, in the life of a computer-based instructional system would probably be as follows: from 8:00 a.m. to 3:00 p.m. the children are exposed to the instructional terminals as an adjunct to the classroom situation. The instructional terminals look like teletypes, which seem satisfactory for the basic drill-and-practice modes, or include television screens and slide projectors for the presentation of video information such as is necessary for both the tutorial and dialogue modes.

At the end of the regular school day, the instructional terminals are employed for remedial work when a child has missed school or has been having difficulty with a particular concept; they are also used for special projects for the bright child who is able to advance at a faster rate than his classroom peers. These types of activities fill most of the afternoon.

In the evening, the entire process is essentially repeated for adult groups or for vocational training. Finally, during the rest of the night, the computer is employed to perform administrative functions that are necessary to maintain the operation of a school system.

CONCLUSION

In considering these facets of computer-assisted instruction, we have only scanned the possible uses of a computer system in the education process. For example, we have not looked at the impact of such a system on a library, where we can certainly anticipate the use of a computer to respond to an individual's request by identifying appropriate source materials and indicating their status and location. Furthermore, we should at least mention the application of a computer-based instructional system to the general problem of vocational guidance and consultation. Guidance systems can be configured, using a computer as the information source.

One other very promising utilization of a computer-based instruction is its application to special groups. These include not only remedial education, but also their application to the education of our mentally handicapped children. The problems of educating a handicapped or emotionally disturbed child usually necessitate a one-to-one ratio between teacher and student. As a consequence large numbers of such children go without any appreciable help and, under the best conditions, receive only minimal guidance. The use of an instructional terminal, therefore, as a teacher surrogate offers a most promising approach to resolving this dilemma.

Finally, we have not discussed the applications of computer-based instruction to higher education. The growing interest in the development of junior colleges, for example, which will potentially offer an additional two years of tuition-free education to all children, imposes a tremendous burden on our teacher population. Once again, it would seem quite reasonable to employ the computer for presenting educational materials as a supplementary device to the classroom situation.

The role, therefore, of the computer in the educational process obviously can not be fully defined at this time. It is apparent that as we experiment with curriculum materials, student groups, and educational facilities, we will recognize more and more applications. There is no denying the fact, however, that the computer has a role to play in the educational process and that this role will become increasingly more significant with each succeeding year.

Technology: The Medium, Not the Message

Leonard A. Muller

A MACHINE IS simply a physical device. The style of education it makes possible is entirely dependent upon the needs, the imagination, the goals, and, above all, the social and human values of the educators who find ways to use the technology.

What the overall shape of things will be as a result of advanced technology is unpredictable at this time. As a businessman, I believe that business can only provide a stimulus to a great and challenging adventure. The final results will depend on the contributions made at every level of education.

It is not necessary to catalogue the advantages and disadvantages of technology. It suffices to say that we must recognize that technology is no panacea — it has built-in limitations, and it creates problems. If we recognize that it is a Janus with two faces, we are in a much better position to seize the opportunities it promises while minimizing the problems it creates. Technology is, after all, only a tool.

The spirit that moves the tool is not in the tool but in ourselves. Some people say that the tool — the medium — is the message, but I say that the medium has no message. Recognizing this, technology in education must be seen only as a means of extending our abilities to teach and multiplying our resources of communicating the human values that make this society and this planet more livable and decent.

You have all been exposed to many of the tools in the spectrum of educational technology. I am going to focus attention specifically on computers because computers have become a symbol of modern technology. They have also been the focus of much fear, of much hope, and of much bewilderment.

COMPUTER CAPABILITIES

Like other technologies, the computer is a tool — an extension of ourselves. However, the extraordinary thing about a computer is that it appears to be an extension of what has always been considered unique in man — his mental operations. This does not mean that it actually duplicates these mental operations; actually, it only simulates them.

First, it can store information, and, therefore, it simulates memory. Second, it can compare one piece of information with another to determine whether something is or is not, whether it is zero or one. Thus, it simulates logical decision-making. Third, it can store symbols — numbers and groups of numbers — that represent external phenomena. Thus, it simulates reality.

In addition, the operations of the machine can be controlled by a previously written set of instructions — stored in the machine, and written by human beings — in such a manner that the machine can actually change its own course of action depending upon what happens during the course of its operations. For example, by instructing the machine not to repeat an operation that produces a certain result, the machine can proceed through a problem by trial and error. This suggests a wide range of roles the machine can play in the educational process.

Ideally the computer should be used in the whole educational system, not only in administration. For example, the use of the computer in such areas as grade reporting, class scheduling and school accounting are already established. The need, of course, will be to orchestrate the capabilities of the computer to the needs of a complicated educational environment.

It is here, in determining relative needs, relative values, and relative importance of the educational functions, that creative innovation will be needed. It is here we should ask, "What can the machine do better than I can do? What, if the machine gives me time, can I do better?"

You have heard a great deal of talk about computer-assisted instruction (CAI), the use of a computer as a tutorial device. The utilization of computers for CAI seems to stir up the most enthusiasm, resentment, and public notice.

There is good reason for this. Because many forms of presentation can be used — image projectors, earphones, typewriters, cathode ray tubes — and because many pupils can work in concert at many different stations tied into the computer, many pupils can interact simultaneously with the machine on an individual basis. Quite literally, the machine is handling these operations one step at a time, but it is handling them internally at speeds of a few millionths of a second. When two children push separate buttons or type out a word, the machine's responses to each pupil may be different, but the responses are, in effect, simultaneous. The same thing can be said if there are twenty, thirty, or more pupils working at as many different instruction stations.

This explains the enthusiasm, perhaps excessive enthusiasm, that so many have expressed about CAI: namely, that it may bring into reality the dream of individualizing instruction in mass education. However, we must remember that CAI is only one way to accomplish this goal and, more importantly, there must be an intelligent mixture of individualized and group instruction. By overstressing computer-assisted instruction, we tend to obscure other important uses now being developed — uses that can be applied immediately with much less effort, cost, and controversy. Nonetheless, a great promise exists in this area.

This brief description projects a picture of twenty, thirty, perhaps hundreds of children in some mechanized room, each sitting in front of his little teaching machine, each receiving the instruction that his capacity demands. One might think this is a pretty dehumanized picture.

Where is the teacher? Is he, freed at last from marking test papers and routine jobs, now merely a disciplinarian, a proctor, or a technician for a pupil who mixes up his buttons? Is he, with all this time on his hands, only checking out the school cafeteria accounts or making an inventory of the Radio Club's equipment? Or is he spending this time with individual students in guidance and counseling, exploring and interpreting with them their learning experience in a way he has never been able to do before?

I can only leave this to you. We do not know the unpredictable ways you will use your machines. What style, what richness — or lack of it — your imagination will supply is unknown at this time.

In stressing how fast a computer operates, how many people it can reach, and the amount of work it can do, one thing is often overlooked. It is that all of these things add up to a great gift, the gift of time. In certain sectors of our society, we have already discovered that the computer can provide freedom from routine tasks and freedom from drudgery, so that we have more time to think, to imagine, to explore old ideas and new ones, more time to evaluate our efforts and our values, and more time to be creative.

DANGERS OF NEW TECHNOLOGY

I have stressed two important things: (1) the computer as a technological innovation, and (2) the responsibility of the educator for educational innovation. We should now examine some of the dangers in applying this new technology. For one thing, the machine has limitations. To ignore them could lead to serious mistakes.

Robert Hutchins has warned us that if we do not recognize the machine's limitations, we could conceivably produce an academic depression rather than stimulate an academic boom. I share this concern, not because I believe machines will depress education but because the misuse of them could.

The computer is a masterful tool for handling measurable data, but it simply has no way of handling values or qualities, affections or attitudes. How does one measure an attitude? Except within a limited scope, as it is programed by a human being, a computer is absolutely indifferent to subtle shades of literary values, nuances of meaning, individual creativity, or individual enterprise. It is a machine, not a teacher. It cannot inspire a student to greatness, nor can it substitute for the personal relations between student and teacher or any other human being. Your pupils may have a favorite teacher; they will never have a favorite computer.

There is another limitation on the use of the computer. Its performance can never be any better than the program and the information we feed into it. For example, when we stimulate in the machine, our results can only be as good as the model we build into the machine. Mathematical models are really only abstractions of reality. Abstractions are notoriously rigid, and they often rule out the spontaneous and the unexpected — two important characteristics of nature and human behavior.

The computer is a powerful tool for analyzing great masses of data, but, to receive a meaningful answer from the machine, we are first obliged to ask the right questions. If we ask the wrong question, we will still get an answer, but the right answer to the wrong question is hardly satisfactory. Asking the right questions and putting the right information into the machine are essential. This is the problem of programing, preparing the software to go into the hardware.

This effort will require new combinations of talent. The traditional author-teacher must be supported by technical people who can translate the language of life into the language of computers. This does not mean that a teacher must know in detail how a computer works. He needs only to know what a computer can do and how to tell it what to do. This too is an opportunity. The history of technology teaches us that those who learn to master it experience an expansion, not a reduction, of their professional roles.

Machines can be misused. Misuse of any technology almost invariably occurs when the people for whom the machine is intended as a tool and a benefit, either for lack of time, for lack of information, or through simple timidity, default on their opportunities and leave it all to the technicians. Technicians, good people though they are, have a primary interest in making machines and organizations go as quietly and efficiently as possible. The primary interest of a teacher, and of education itself, is the transmission of information and values to develop human beings and to enhance the quality of individual lives.

Only the teacher has that intuitive sense of what can be turned to instructional purposes, that inner feeling for what an individual or class can absorb. These qualities, plus the teacher's sense of situation, like an athlete or actor's, makes him the essential link between student and machine. At best, the teacher has the greatest potential as a source of educational innovations that will make the technological tools useful and creative. At the least, the teacher is the necessary brake on technological innovation that, like any use of machines, can become dehumanized if efficiency is allowed to become an end in itself.

ROLE OF BUSINESS AND GOVERNMENT IN EDUCATION

Related to the dangers of striving for over-efficiency are the dangers of over-control. In the past few years, we have seen the entry of large industry or big business into the field of education. We have also seen "big government" enter education in that the federal government has become a major source of funds for local school systems. In our time, state government is also big government as a major source of support for local school systems. You know how many items in a local school budget are mandated by the state educational agency.

In general the consensus appears to be that this is good and necessary to produce uniform and quality education. At the same time, however, American education has been proud, and has reason to be proud, of its relative autonomy in society and in its historic ability to respond to local needs.

But computer technology is expensive, and big government has more money than local school systems. What, then, is the possibility of big business aligning itself with big government, state or federal, to make big sales that might possibly result in one big program that abolishes local autonomy entirely and provides us with one uniform educational program from nursery school through retraining for retirement?

This may be a gross exaggeration, but there is a real danger here. On the other hand, we do have a number of strong safeguards. First, our very awareness of this possible danger makes it less probable. Second, business, whose performance is always subject to the acid test of competition, will introduce a healthy force in the overall arrangement of checks and balances. Third, and very importantly, we have great protection against the imposition, however well-intentioned it might be, of undesired uniformity and conformity because of the very diversity of the educational system itself and, added to this, the diversity of the various governments and businesses involved.

ROLE OF EDUCATORS IN USING TECHNOLOGY

The greatest deterrent against the spectre of big business and big government control will be early, positive participation by educators in the use of the emerging technologies. We are at a cross roads today similar to that facing the nation at the turn of the century in transportation. At that time the vast majority of intellectuals, who would later be deeply affected by the automobile, stood passively on the side lines, either skeptical or antagonistic. Had they participated then in examining the implications of this new tool, we might well be free of the current problems of air pollution, traffic safety, and road planning. So if the educators, recognizing the weaknesses and limitations of the machine, step in now and become actively enthusiastic participants in this innovation, the same mistake can be avoided and control of this system can remain firmly in the hands of the educators.

Of course, I can't speak for government or for education; I can only speak as a businessman and can only suggest to you that here is a powerful technological tool. It may shake up some of your old beliefs, and it may make you a little uncomfortable at times. But it will also help you cope with powerful forces that challenge and even threaten you: the acceleration of change, the ever-increasing numbers of people to be educated, the flood of new information, and the urgent appeal for equality and excellence. Put this device on your educational edifice because it holds great promise for helping you meet these problems.

As businessmen we cannot know what kind of an educational edifice you are intending to put our technological device on. This is really still locked up in the endless diversity of the imaginations of individual educators and teachers and in the endless diversity of the localities and the regions of our nation. We, however, are not just going to sell our gadget and pass on. We will provide you with extensive technical support. We are not selling some sort of all-purpose magic but a machine that must be adapted and programed for the individual use of the individual educational system. We businessmen cannot determine the ends of education; but business has resources that should not be overlooked by educators. If I have any advice to give you, it is a two-fold suggestion.

First, there are some computer uses today that have proved to be effective in education and demand immediate attention. Specifically, certain data needs to be compiled, analyzed, and evaluated to provide a better picture of what is happening in the schools. The technical support exists to aid in accomplishing this now. There are also other established uses of computers that should be examined for possible inclusion in an overall plan for the school, notably problem-solving, simulation, and the other uses mentioned.

Second, educators should watch closely the developments in the more experimental areas, such as CAI, that will offer great opportunities for research or meeting special needs.

If educators do not begin these tasks, someone else might. It would be tragic if the final word did not come from those who are finally responsible — the teachers and administrators close to the classroom.

Thus, there is a great challenge before us today: the challenge to secure the benefits of technology without losing our sense of continuity and without compromising the integrity of our educational system or the integrity of the one individual it is intended to serve — the student.

The job will be difficult, but the promise is too great to let the difficulty deter us. In the words of Walter Lippman:

> We must measure not by what it would be easy and convenient to do but by what it is necessary to do in order that the nation may survive and flourish. We have learned that we are quite rich enough to defend ourselves, whatever the cost. We must now learn that we are quite rich enough to educate ourselves as we need to be educated.

Humanistic Technology

John Henry Martin

WHAT IS THE COMPUTER from an educator's point of view? The computer is a distant brain we hope will be useful to education. For it to be useful to education, it has to arrive at a point where it and a student can communicate.

Two factors have delayed the development of computer-assisted instruction. One is the revelation that comes from an examination of the semantics of the language of the computer. We are still calling the point where education is to begin a "terminal." Similarly, we use the term "multi-media." These are both engineer-orientated terms. Since educators think of human senses, it would be more appropriate to talk about the computer as a beginning point, rather than as a terminal. Furthermore, we should not be speaking in terms of multi-media; we should instead be speaking of multi-sensory learning — utilization of all the learner's senses in the activities of education.

The second factor that has hampered, and is continuing to hamper, computer-assisted instruction is its excessive reliance on one narrow base of learning theory. That narrow base, Skinner Programmatic Design, is only a fragment of the learning theory. Skinner's contribution can be likened to that of one of the six blind men in the ancient Hindu fable, who all stroked an elephant and touched it at a different point. Each investigator of human behavior who is involved in acquiring information or new insight typically touches an extremely powerful mechanism.

Thus Skinner utilizes only one facet of human behavior — a complex of information or skills is broken down and given to the learner in parts, in a carefully controlled situation, and the learner is then instantly rewarded for each success. As a result of this sequence, a higher order of learning and retention of the information is achieved. Now that is good, fine, and true, but it is not the "whole elephant" of human behavior involved in learning.

Yet computer-based instruction has seized that particular facet of learning theory and has utilized it alone in programing for the computer, as though this were the only capability of the computer and the only way human beings could be taught or could learn from it.

EDUCATIONAL REQUIREMENTS FOR COMPUTERS

There is then an excessive reliance on engineering terms in referring to computers and an excessive reliance on a too narrow base of learning theory. We do not, of course, know all the facets of learning theory, but we do have a number of significant additional insights into this theory. One aspect we have known for a long time — if the learner uses more than one of his senses simultaneously and concurrently in a planned orchestration of his involvement, his learning will be of a higher degree than if he uses a single sense. His retention will also be greater, and his speed of acquisition will be faster. Yet the terminals now used in education are ones in which the only sensory involvement is that of the eye.

What is the reason for this emasculation of the terminal, this failure to see it as the beginning point of learning? Educators are not demanding the type of equipment they need.

What educators want from a terminal or a learning center is a behavior of instrumentation that closely approximates the behavior of the human being in a tutorial relationship to another human being. This means that we need instrumentation that will talk, that will listen, and that will present pictorially graphic material, symbolic material, and printed prose. We need an instrument that will permit the learner to intercede at each point in such presentations, one that will then change its presentations accordingly. If the computer is to be reduced to a page-turner for a workbook, then it is not needed. It must be something more than a teletype machine clattering at a child in drill sessions. It must be an instrument that focuses on how a human being behaves when he learns and how he can be stimulated to behave in sequences that utilize all of his senses.

READING AS A CRUCIAL AREA

Another problem in today's use of technology in education is the poverty of the programing for it. Superior programing must be designed to meet the needs of the single most difficult aspect of American education — in terms of present performance level — the teaching of reading. The evidence is that in the inner cities of the United States, we are not teaching children to read. The failure rate is so high and so excessive, that if we were a corporation, we would be declared bankrupt. At the end of the first grade in the inner city, only about 25 per cent of the children read at grade level, which means that they have achieved a 175-word recognition level at the end of the sixth year of life.

On the current scene, there are at least 22 variants of methods to correct this situation. Each has a contribution to make, each has its advocates, and each has achieved some success; but the present methodology of teaching reading in the cities of the United States is a bankrupt methodology. Individual teachers who have the unique drive, concern, and a high degree of personal relationship with the particular children involved do accomplish reversals of this trend, but the system as a whole has failed.

Therefore, we need a new methodology, whether it happens to be technology or a new instructional process. In any case the instructional processes now used are ineffective. Any process that produces a 75 per cent failure rate at six years of life should be seen for what it is — a horrible psychological blow, a root-cause of all subsequent academic failures, and a root-cause of all subsequent deviation from social norms.

If a child at six learns that he cannot master the one entry to the world of the human race, then at six years of age we are teaching him that he does not belong to that world. Therefore, we should not be surprised that the disadvantaged child is more impaired eight years later than he would have been with no schooling at all.

READING TECHNOLOGY

One of the technological aids used to improve this situation is the talking typewriter. The Responsive Environment Corporation has designed for this machine a software methodology to assist in this most critical, difficult, and confused area in American education. This software consists of two sets of programatic design material for reading. Hundreds of four- to six-year-olds have completed this program successfully, reversing the 75-to-25 failure-to-success ratio. Through this program, at the end of four months, five-year-olds are reading at a level not yet achieved by a control group one year older at the end of the first grade.

In this program textbooks are used that emphasize city scenes — the environment of the children — and have a vocabulary density double to that of the normal standard reading program.

In addition, we have tried to operate within the framework of the total educational system. We have studied the organizational results of introducing technology in education and have found that in the typical educational system, the teacher can become competitive with and hostile to technology.

Considering this fact, we have reversed the system. The teacher is not competitive with the instrument; the teacher is a part of the system. The children go from the classroom to the center, spend their 15-minute sessions at the instrument, and leave the instrument with a tearsheet that is a complete record of every stroke made and every action taken by the youngster. The child thus returns to the classroom with so individualized a record as to mandate individualized instruction by the teacher.

After a period of days, the physical evidence of the differences between the children makes it impossible for the teacher to return to mass-group instruction or even small-group instruction, which is at best but an ineffective substitute that merely moves away from 30 at a time to 5-to-7 at a time, instead of one at a time, which is the essential need. With the use of standard curricula materials in harmony with the technological reading program of the instrument, the progress rate from child to child, from instrument to instrument, from day to day, is a completely individualized affair.

It is essential to coordinate the roles of teacher and machine; it is also desirable to involve the community in these centers. Children can be monitored and observed by trained laymen as teacher aides. The center is thus planned so that the child, his classmates, his teacher, his curriculum, and his school system are all integral parts of one carefully systematized programing development. This system has proved to be a very successful way of utilizing technology in the school system to facilitate greater learning.

To expedite greater use of such technology then, we must first think of computers in educational rather than engineering terms. We must tell the manufacturers what our needs are. And we cannot limit the use of technology to one facet of the learning process. Further, we must apply technology to our most crucial educational problems, such as the teaching of reading, and we must apply it effectively through the use of the appropriate software methodology — programing — for each particular problem. Finally, we must always remember to incorporate technology in the system in such a way that it is a meaningful part of the teacher-pupil-community relationship, rather than a disparate element. Only by carefully considering these factors can we utilize technology to improve substantially the quality of education.

Technological Tools: Flexible and Efficient

Richard H. Bell

MODERN TECHNOLOGY in general, and television in particular, is a flexible and efficient tool for education, a means of organizing, storing, and transmitting experience, and it is an essential tool in today's world. If we were starting today to develop an educational system, we would think it inconceivable to develop such a system without making basic use of the many advantages offered us by modern technology.

To emphasize this point, I would ask you to project many years into the future and from that vantage point think back to the imaginary day we invented education. This will take a bit of doing for, as you recall, that was way back in 1967. Permit me to refresh your memories about the status of our civilization in that summer of 1967.

We had an affluent society in the United States. Never had so many people enjoyed so many of the good things of life. We had a strong centralized federal government, which could take effective action in areas of its choice, action that would influence the entire nation and its people. We also had a rapidly expanding population that threatened grave over-crowding in America and critical over-crowding in the world by the year 2000. And, since 1900, we had developed the most highly advanced technology the world had ever known. Technically, nearly anything was possible. Moreover, we had a body of knowledge that had doubled three times since the turn of the 20th century.

But we had no formal education. Of course people had been learning for some five thousand years. We could not have advanced as we did without learning. Learning had proved to be a natural condition of man, but never had society attempted to structure a system whereby the culture of the past could be transmitted to the new generation. Never had we felt it necessary to develop a system to teach new skills to the young, to teach them how to appreciate, to learn, to think.

By the summer of 1967, however, the government had decided that it was time to develop a system to accomplish these goals. People were fearful about the future, were uncomfortable living with change, and were perhaps a little frightened by their freedom and its concomitant responsibilities.

So the president appointed the now-famous National Commission for the Invention of Education. A White House Conference was held, out of which came committees to develop this new social structure from the standpoints of goals and objectives, methods, tests and measurements, administration, financing and cost effectiveness, and strategy.

STRATEGY OF LEARNING

The report of the Strategy Committee is my topic. This group had submitted a dual report. These two conflicting reports have since joined the professional literature as the Trump Plan and the No-Trump Plan, and it is interesting to look at them in historical perspective now that so many years have elapsed since 1967.

It was assumed from the outset that one tactical problem of this new system known as education would be that of bringing the learner into contact with learning material, and two opposing solutions were proposed.

The No-Trump Report proposed bringing all students together in various central locations where the learning material could be presented to them. It was argued that this would be easier for the teachers, who could disseminate verbally the results of their years of study to the learners through a system that would be known as a "lecture" — derived from a word "lecterne," meaning a wooden box behind which a lecturer could take refuge so he would not have to come into intimate contact with the learners.

It was recognized that these groups would have to be divided in some way for ease of handling, and it was apparent that the simplest approach would be to divide them into age groups so the teacher could be trained to teach children of the same age. When the objection was raised that similarly aged students might be quite disparate in their interests and abilities, the No-Trump Group answered that a good teacher could motivate them to become interested in those things in which the teacher, in her infinite wisdom, knew they should be interested.

The Trump Report, on the other hand, proposed taking the learning materials to the student, wherever he might be. This would mean that the learner could work directly with learning materials in the form of books, recorded audio material, visual material in various forms, and the real objects of the world. In some cases this learning material would be presented by master presenters, a specialized branch of the teaching profession whose exciting performances could be recorded on video tape, film, and whatever other new devices for visual storage and display might be invented. Further, since computer technology was far advanced, it was immediately seen that learning material could be organized in this configuration to allow maximum individual adaptability for each learner.

As for the problem of grouping, it was seen by this committee that since the learners were human beings, it would be better to allow the individual to pursue different learning objectives at his own pace, making rapid progress in some areas and taking more time in those in which he had less interest and proficiency. Through a variety of alternatives, each student could pursue more deeply fields in his own particular interest-areas in which he had a natural interest and motivation.

In structuring the learning materials, it was apparent to the Trump Committee that the systems approach used by technology and industry held promise as a way in which to design material in a sequential fashion that would enable the learner, whether as an individual or in a group, to progress in a systematic, effective manner to a predetermined behavioral objective. The No-Trump Group, on the other hand, assumed that if a teacher were placed in the classroom and permitted to talk long enough, he would cover the important information, and the student would become "more well-rounded" or a "richer person" in the process.

In this regard, the No-Trump Report insisted that something educational would happen by virtue of the teacher and learner being in the same room with one another. But the Trump Group took what has since become known as a "multi-media approach," whereby the technological device best designed for a specific learning objective would be used at that point in the educational process. In teaching music, for instance, tapes of excellent musical performances would be used instead of the teacher singing it all. In presenting science demonstrations, video tape would be used and reused, giving an excellent and easily visible demonstration to the students, either in groups or on individual call through a dial-access system. When the learners were adult and it was difficult to bring them together for a learning situation, the teacher could be sent to them electronically through television, coming into the home, school, or factory where they were located. When the student was seeking answers to questions of his own choosing, a computer could be programed to provide answers and alternative lines of development that would vary with the answers.

For the problem of skill development, the No-Trumpers proposed having the learner perform the skill and then be told by the teacher whether he had performed it well or poorly. The Trump Report, on the other hand, could see no reason why the student should not be recorded on audio or video tape as he performed aural or visual skills and then see himself performing while discussing his performance with his instructor.

By such use of technology in the educational tasks for which it was most effective, it was obvious that learners would have more time for interaction with each other and that the teachers would have more time for work with individual students and small groups since all teachers would not be presenters of material. These other teachers, who would be skilled in working with learners, would be in another field of specialization in the teaching profession. They would be known as learner leaders, or learning managers.

Since education was to be based on learning, it was felt that the learner should seek answers to questions that were important to him, using a wide variety of human and technical resources to help him arrive at answers as a result of a thinking process, rather than having education consist of giving him predetermined answers for all questions.

As we know, all this is history, and we can all be grateful that it was obvious to everyone that the only system that made sense in our modern society was that proposed by the Trump Report. Admittedly some students would have learned under the No-Trump Plan, but it was apparent that the quantitative and qualitative tasks of education were so vast in the mid-20th century, that we could ill afford to ignore any devices, equipment, approaches, or techniques that could facilitate maximum learning by the greatest number of students.

TELEVISION

But obvious as this is, let me warn you that there are among us those who would prefer to have education shift to a doing-it-by-hand system on the pretext that it is easier, cheaper, better, or more humanistic. To arm you against such a temptation, may I take but one technological medium — television — and review its contributions to the educative process.

First, television can transmit reality with a vividness that matches reality itself. Further, this can be structured reality, permitting the viewer a better view of the event in a more understandable fashion than if he were actually present. Through editing, choice of location, varied points of view, and interpretive narration, television can be used to structure reality into a learning experience.

Television can also multiply the dissemination of experience, making it available to a great number of learners in many different locations. Moreover, through its power to magnify the very small, television can increase visibility and enhance the possibility of learning.

With the use of the video-tape recorder, television can record and store experiences, enabling the learner to tap that experience when he needs it in his own educational development. In this way television can be used, not just as a mass medium, but as a device for individualized instruction. Furthermore, video tape provides the most efficient and effective device for recording human behavior that we have developed to date. Behavior is recorded, stored, and displayed, enabling us to study the human being in action in a most effective manner.

By avoiding duplication of presentations, television can relieve some teachers of this function, thus enabling them to spend more time with students. This permits the teacher to become what he should be — the structurer of learning experiences for individual students rather than an information storage and retrieval device.

There is an appropriate and economically feasible television configuration to meet a wide variety of educational needs. A thousand dollar system can be used to increase learning in the classroom. A one-half million dollar educational television station can provide learning experiences for hundreds and thousands of students in an entire city or state, thus spreading the base and creating a system that is reasonable on a unit-cost basis. The present high cost of television is a result of the high cost of mistakes such as purchasing the wrong equipment for a designated educational task.

None of these points implies that television improves the learner, that it replaces the teacher, or that it revolutionizes education. But, television is an excellent educational tool that we would most certainly utilize if we were to "invent" education today.

As we learn more about learners, about the learning process, and about technology, we will find more uses for television in education. As education changes, we will be able to use television more effectively in the teaching-learning process. As we free our thinking and become true innovators, we will use television in instruction more creatively than we have in the past, and we will use it, not as a field of its own and not as ETV per se, but as a system that is a fundamental part of educational technology, which itself must be an integral part of the educative endeavor.

There is no reason why we should wait for the perfection of technology or for the so-called "revolution in education." Television, along with other products of modern technology, can be used efficiently right now. The question of whether it will be an effective aid to education or just another educational fad rests in your hands. It is no panacea, nor is it a frill or a gadget. It is another tool in the hands of the skilled educator.

Forty years ago, Stephen Vincent Benét, in his epic American poem "John Brown's Body," viewed the beginning of the growth of modern technology, and he saw with great insight human reactions to it. He refers to the period as "the engine-handed age" and to technology as "the genie we have raised to rule the earth." His final words in the poem are applicable to educators today:

> And while the prophets shudder or adore
> Before the flame, hoping it will give ear,
> If you at last must have a word to say,
> Say neither, in their way,
> "It is a deadly magic and accursed,"
> Nor "It is blest," but only "It is here."

Modern technology is, indeed, here. Either it will control us, or we will control it. The outcome is still in doubt, and the outcome is in your hands. It is up to you.

The Potential Educational Impact of Television

John B. Burns

TELEVISION IS A MAJOR ASPECT of life in the United States. You have all heard and read the statistics of television's dimensions: the television set in the average American home is in use more than five and one half hours every day of the year, and television reaches 95 per cent of all homes. Almost all this viewing, however, is of commercial television. ETV, educational television, reaches only 10 per cent of American homes for less than one and one-half hours per week.

On one hand, there is commercial TV that has, in two decades, become the most successful communications medium of all time. On the other hand, there is ETV. Compared with the growth and success of commercial television, ETV has stagnated. ETV has not succeeded in playing an important part in the educational process. It has not lived up to its hopes and expectations.

Ambitious plans are being proposed to bring new life to ETV. These plans suggest that spending of hundreds of millions of dollars will bring a solution. The current debate concerns the manner in which this money can be obtainable and organization of the system.

What has not been done, however, is to analyze the particular power of commercial television to see what lessons it affords for educational television. While the foundations acknowledge that commercial television has a small percentage of good and worthwhile programing, they equate worthwhile programing with information and cultural programing. There is no suggestion that anything can be learned from the regular programing of commercial television, the entertainment programs. This omission stems from the negative evaluation of commercial television by those outside commercial broadcasting.

CRITICISMS OF COMMERCIAL TELEVISION

From the beginning television has been the victim of many misconceptions that, at first, seemed plausible. Not too long ago, people honestly believed that television was bad for the eyes. More recently it was believed that television was not so bad for the eyes if another light were on in the room. It was also generally accepted that watching television would stunt children's growth and give them bad posture, that it would take the place of reading, and that it would stifle the art of conversation. Some of those misconceptions are no longer with us; others still exist, but to a smaller degree.

For instance, as recently as 1961 the writers of *Television in the Lives of Our Children* grouped children in classes. The first class contained the children who watched television frequently and seldom read. This group was called the "fantasy group." The second class contained children who read frequently and seldom watched television; these children were called the "reality group." The purpose of the writers was to present an objective appraisal. However, our society is so print-oriented that these writers began with the preconception that reading is, of course, good and connected with reality. Television is connected with fantasy; and fantasy is bad.

The writers also stated that, "indeed, the most likely social effect of television is no effect." In 1961 viewing time was more than five hours per television-home per day, and then, as now, the overwhelming majority of all households in the

United States had television. To assume that this tremendous amount of television viewing would not have a social effect is an untenable position. But then these writers did not even see television as a separate medium; they saw it as radio with a new, visual dimension.

The writers were also afraid that adult life, as portrayed on television, might give a biased view of the adult world. But isn't every family with whom children live biased in one or another? Aren't books, even the best, biased? *The Brothers Karamazov* hardly presents an unbiased view of the world, nor does *Huckleberry Finn* or *Main Street*.

But books are favored because they have an "information" content. It is in this regard that we have to look at television as compared with formal school education. School puts great stress on facts and information, comprehension and understanding.

Should television play the same role in our lives? Does television have to teach what is now being taught in classrooms, just as computers seemingly are being programed to help classroom instruction? Or should television be used to teach what is not taught in classrooms or support what is being taught in classrooms?

To find the answers to these questions, it is first necessary to recognize television for what it is. Only in this way, can we find out what television can possibly do for education. One has to accept the fact that commercial television supports itself by its ability to attract a mass audience. No matter how everyone may think television ought to be programed, the point that really matters is that television is being used successfully.

NATURE OF TELEVISION AS A MEDIUM

There are two aspects of television that need clarification: (1) the nature of the medium, and (2) the content of that medium, the programing itself.

While it is the content, the programing of television that I want to stress, understanding the nature of the medium is a necessary base for the production of programs. This is true whether we produce commercial or educational programs, but must we differentiate between the two types of programing? Do commercial programs and educational programs have to be different? A connection may already exist between formal education and television.

Herbert J. Gans, in his article in the *Urban Review* on the mass media as an educational institution, points out that both the schools and the media prepare children for adult society. By letting children attend adult courses, mass media give the child great opportunity for preparation for adulthood, although the media do not train people in specific skills. Schools emphasize skills and ideals; the media emphasize the actualities of life.

According to Gans, media, as well as the schools, select and distort in describing America — the media by emphasizing the dramatic and the unusual; the schools by stressing the abstract and traditional. Both media and the schools seek to perpetuate American culture. While the schools promote the 19th century lower-middle-class tradition of the small town, media encourage the 20th century non-Puritan culture. An outcome of this difference in viewpoint, according to Gans, is that the school considers mass media uncultured, while the mass media view the school as dull, stodgy, and unfashionable.

Gans also points out that the schools need pay very little attention to audience dissatisfaction, while this is of major concern to media. However, schools are subject to many problems that do not trouble media, such as equalization and integration, and schools have to deal with external agencies to obtain money. Further, they work with tenured professionals who tend to be conservative, and they have to bend to the ideas of the universities and to the conservative opinions of adult society as to what the content of instruction should be. Perhaps they also should ask what they can learn from the mass media.

In the *New Yorker,* Pauline Kael, the movie critic, pointed out that our perspective on a medium can change in the short period of a generation. She was discussing movies of the 30's and 40's. By critical standards, she said, most would be classed as having little value, yet they probably taught those who grew up with them more about the world and values than did formal education. Those movies helped make one generation aware. Similarly, Reverend Louis Reile of St. Mary's University in San Antonio, recently said that films are the textbook of the contemporary man.

In much the same way, television is the textbook of teen-agers and children, not the clearly defined informational and educational programs of television, but the commercial programs — the programs that are so readily dismissed by critics as entertainment and escapist fare. It is true that the most obvious fact about television is that it entertains, but if we assume that Americans watch television as much as they do only to be entertained, we are explaining the truth by selecting only the most obvious aspect. Let us look at television as more than an entertainment medium to see what else it contributes.

CONTENT OF COMMERCIAL PROGRAMING

Those programs that present dramatic situations in the lives of different people — doctors, policemen, and so forth —deal with human relationships, responsibility, initiative, judgment, and personal freedom. They are concerned with intuition, the will, values of experience, moral standards, and the complexity of human beings and human behavior. Some of these dramatic programs present pertinent moral issues or magnify human relationships under the tensions of a crisis situation. In short, these programs dramatize lessons of life that are not part of a formal curriculum.

Other types of programs satisfy different needs. For instance, situation comedies are often directed toward gratification of the desire for security and emotional relief of tension. Variety shows deal with aspects of creativity in the performing arts.

Commercial television, if viewed in this way, does have an educational content. Its relationship to formal education as presented in schools is comparable to much other education a child acquires outside the school. A child learns to speak and walk without formal education. When a child plays, he educates himself; ball playing, bicycling, and hop-scotch teach, among other things, balance, depth-perception, coordination, and interaction with other children. Playing and television-viewing are both pleasurable. That does not mean they are not educational. These are methods of informal education in the sense that they teach children to become well-functioning members of adult society.

The entertainment aspect of television, then, is only the umbrella beneath which a host of other elements are presented to the viewer. The entertainment aspect of television is scorned by critics. They cannot realize or do not want to realize that entertainment is only a way of presenting content in a manner that involves the viewer and keeps him interested.

Watching television is also regarded as mere escapism — the viewer's attempt to escape from reality. But is it?

MGM recently started a research project to find out what the attitude of children is toward cartoon shows. From this research, we have found that a television program must satisfy basic human needs to be acceptable. To find out what those needs are, we turned to the audience.

For instance, much has been said and written about violence on television and the harmful effect it has on children. We listened to the children; we learned that they, in general, regard themselves as weak and see themselves as living in a world full of compulsions — "Do this" — and restrictions — "Don't do that." Whether they want to or not, they are forced by their parents and society to behave in a cerain way. Whether they want to or not, they have to go to school where they have little choice in what they learn. Adults have a tendency to regard childhood as a time of freedom from worries. Children don't feel free at all; they feel hemmed-in, frustrated, and powerless. Our research indicated that the child needs outlets for this pent-up frustration and will be aggressive and negative in varying degrees without such outlets. Cartoons present a great deal of violence, but we learned that it is of a nature that appeals to the child — the underdog overcomes the villain, but nobody really gets hurt. The violence takes place without any serious consequences and without any guilt feelings. Thus, the preconceived notion that all violence per se is bad is not necessarily true. It is not true, of course, that all portrayal of violence is good, but the presentation of violence without consequences seems to be beneficial.

At the same time, we found that children have a great sense about what is real and what is not real. Children know that bunnies do not talk and that the cartoon Bugs Bunny is unreal. However, he looks like a bunny and eats bunny food, and that is real. In fact, it is the juxtaposition of reality and fantasy in cartoons that is a source of satisfaction and fun for most children.

Moreover, cartoons can serve to relieve the child of fears by showing the fearful in pleasant ways. Casper, the friendly ghost, was mentioned by children as relieving anxiety about ghosts. Cartoons can provide a sense of security, which is a very real need.

RE-EXAMINATION OF ROLE OF TV IN EDUCATION

The point of these facts and beliefs about television is that a re-examinnation of the role of television in education is needed so that educational television can become an important factor in the learning process. This can happen when we realize that for viewers to tune in voluntarily, the program has to involve them and has to entertain them. This is of paramount importance.

Further, we have to realize that television is not a classroom. We are not really using television if we use it to present a master teacher on the screen. All this does is replace one classroom situation with another which, despite the master teacher, is not necessarily better, since on television there is no feedback situation between teacher and students.

Television could be better employed in education by consciously pursuing a path that now seems to be hidden from view. That path is not the presentation of what is now being taught in schools, certainly not the presentation of facts and information. That is really better done in books, where the student can go back and review something as many times as necessary for understanding, or in the classroom, where the teacher can explain in many different ways, in whatever period of time is needed. Where television can serve formal education is in the presentation of concepts, forms, shapes, ideas, and relationships. If educators know what they want to present in this area of education, entertainment programs can be produced that have a planned educational content.

For example, the area of reading presents possibilities for programing. Many pre-schoolers now begin to learn to read by watching cereal commercials, where the spelling is as close to the phonetic as is possible in English. KIX, in cereal language, is spelled K-I-X, not K-I-C-K-S. Also, while the word KIX is spoken, only the letters K-I-X appear on the screen, without any other words that might confuse the child. Children also learn from the cartoon songs that use words and a bouncing ball, and they acquire reading and word comprehension from game shows. These programs are not only entertaining but could well serve as models for other entertainment programs that have a higher educational content.

The main problem, then, in considering the use of television in education stems from the need to eliminate current misconceptions about commercial television programing.

First, the word "escapism," which is often applied to commercial television, is used negatively to signify an escape from reality. Why is this not viewed positively? The escape is not from, but toward something — toward emotional gratification, for one thing. This is certainly an aspect of reality. It is at the heart of people's involvement and participation in television. This involvement is the very real message of the medium.

Secondly, the word "entertainment" projects the idea of a glossy surface with no underlying content of value. This is the usual quick dismissal when critics are looking for educational content, but entertainment is vital to the process of television communication. Entertainment is a way of presentation that attracts an audience on a voluntary basis, but entertainment is not the content. Entertainment serves to make the realities of life palatable and enjoyable.

Television cannot be the environment for formal education of a mass audience but it can be an adjunct — a very real one, once the misconceptions about entertainment and escapism are eliminated. Once this has been accomplished, useful lessons for educators can be learned from commercial television, which is a major facet of life in the United States. A force like this cannot be dismissed with the words "entertainment" and "escapism." A look beneath the surface is necessary. If we try to look deeper, we discover that the entertaining aspects of television attract viewers who see, within this framework, a content that is often educational. It is educational in that it instructs young and adults alike about aspects of life and ways of dealing with these aspects.

Therefore, education, in using television for its own purposes, has to recognize that television is a unique medium, with its own nature and its own special interaction with the audience. To employ television for educational purposes, education must use it to do what it can do best. Utilizing entertainment to attract an audience, educational aims can be pursued. Using television to teach what is now taught in schools has been tried, but it has not been very successful. Therefore, we should consider that television might perform best in areas of education that are not stressed in schools or that television can support what is now taught in schools. One must analyze television for what it is and forget what he thinks it should be.

In utilizing television, educators might look to the makers of commercials. These people have perhaps been the medium's leading innovators. They have mastered the art of video communication — the art of conveying specific information quickly to many people. They have been educators if one acknowledges that teaching people about consumption is a form of education.

Let us recognize, then, that commercial television is a force and that it should be put to more effective use in helping to solve the problems of education. Mere protest against what is inferior will not help; protest does not present solutions. Positive action and definition of goals are required. That is the task of educators who know what is needed. This need should be explicated. The people who are best able to suggest solutions to needs are the young educators now in their early 20's who have been brought up with television. They instinctively know the interrelationships, the strengths, and also the weaknesses of mass television communications. They are the first television generation to come to adulthood. They have known it virtually all their lives. They know its language and can thus utilize it imaginatively.

Finally, we must think of commercial television as a positive force that involves tremendous numbers of people every day without any compulsion. There is general agreement that television can and should play a greater role in the process of education. By applying the principles of commercial television to its own system, the world of education will be expanded and enriched.

Appendix: Ideas for Innovative Programs and Dissemination of Innovations

This summary of I³ Group recommendations was prepared by the Project EDINN staff, of which Edwin C. Coffin is Director and Beatrice Ward is Program Executive. Project EDINN (EDucational INNovation) is a regional educational planning agency serving Monterey, San Benito, and Santa Cruz Counties, California, and is funded under the auspices of ESEA Title III.

The interaction or I³ (Involvement, Identity, and Innovation) groups, composed of 15 to 20 participants who met regularly during each seminar, were asked to develop two major categories of recommendations for the improvement of education: (1) ideas for innovative programs that the U.S. Office of Education and the Kettering Foundation should consider for funding, and (2) ideas concerning methods for disseminating educational innovations, other than the traditional newsletter. Toward these goals, group members became *involved* in thinking about concepts presented at the seminars and in designing new approaches for improving one or more facets of the education program. They *identified* with participants having common interests and concerns — persons from throughout the nation who work as school district superintendents, school principals, PACE project directors, state department of education personnel, and members of the staff of the U.S. Office of Education. Also they considered *innovation* in terms of the "intellectual input" to be absorbed and reacted to by the persons involved and in terms of the "creative output" to emerge from the group and each of its members.

IDEAS FOR INNOVATIVE PROGRAMS

Recommendations for new programs to be funded fall into the following five major categories.

Programs to Support Innovation in Schools

Most of the I³ groups recommended some kind of program that would facilitate innovation within school systems. The majority of these recommendations involved efforts to educate and influence people:

1. Several groups sought means of creating greater support for innovative programs among school board members. The only detailed suggestion about how this might be accomplished was to provide funds for school board members to attend professional conferences at which new programs are discussed.

2. Some I³ groups emphasized projects that would provide leadership training for school administrators and Title III project directors. Programs in sensitivity training were specifically suggested, as were more general workshops in the nature of change and the decision-making process.

3. Other recommendations were less well defined and simply suggested some type of project to learn how to change teacher behavior and how to prepare teachers for change.

In addition to the above comments directed toward preparing various personnel for innovation, the I³ groups suggested a number of other ideas for programs that might facilitate innovation in the schools:

1. The position of "educational catalyst" might be established in school systems, with the person filling the job assuming responsibility for helping school faculties to initiate changes.

2. Teachers' organizations could be involved in making decisions about new programs as a means of enlisting cooperation.

3. Systems specialists might be employed to work with school personnel in analysis of the requirements for change and the means of innovation.

4. Task forces could be established within a region to advise school districts and individual faculties interested in developing or adopting new programs.

5. Projects could be developed to provide assistance to practitioners in translating research findings into implications for new programs.

Programs to Strengthen Pre-service and In-service Education

Almost all the I[3] group reports recommended programs to improve the professional preparation of teachers and other school personnel. Some of these suggestions were sweeping and vague — "Design an entirely new teacher education program which is effective." Others were more concrete; for example, in regard to the continuing education of teachers already in service suggestions were made to:

1. Establish retraining centers apart from the traditional workshops and summer programs sponsored by school districts and universities.

2. Form university teams to go into the schools for intensive education of individual faculties.

3. Set up university sponsored independent study grants for teachers in service.

With respect to pre-service preparation, recommendations included:

1. Establish programs involving extensive cooperation among various agencies — local school districts, universities, Title III centers, and regional educational laboratories.

2. Establish one-year internships as part of the preparation program for both teachers and administrators.

3. Design a school program to improve the supervision of student teachers.

4. Work out various means of orienting professors of education to the operational problems of schools: exchange university and elementary/secondary teachers; include professors in I/D/E/A and Title III seminars; hold briefings by school faculties.

5. Develop ways to give practitioners a substantial role in the design of teacher education programs.

Also falling in the general area of improving the education of school personnel were recommendations that:

1. Local school districts and universities cooperate in designing and conducting programs to prepare paraprofessionals.

2. Internships be provided in Title III projects for graduate education students.

Programs Related to Curriculum Content and Instructional Procedures

Some of the recommendations were related to the broad area of curriculum contents:

1. Plan a curriculum designed to teach various intellectual skills rather than a prescribed body of content.

2. Experiment with a foreign language program in which half of the daily instruction would be in English and the other half in the foreign language.

Several recommendations dealt with instructional media and materials. It was suggested, for example, that a project be funded to establish multi-district instructional media centers. A related suggestion called for county educational television centers to be used both for instruction and for professional communication. One I[3] group suggested that a program be launched to establish standards for technical tools that are used in the classroom, for example, video-tape recorders.

Three other recommendations dealing with instructional media and tools were:

1. Activity or learning packages be prepared as a total system to support continuous progress.

2. A project be developed in which industry and educational agencies cooperate to design sample programs for computer-assisted instruction.

3. The use of technological aids in teaching the arts and humanities be explored.

Other recommendations dealt with the pupil's role in the instructional program: using pupils as tutors and experimenting with ways in which students might assume greater responsibility for planning their own educational programs. Other projects were suggested to:

1. Analyze various kinds of learning experiences in relation to alternative patterns of school and classroom organization in order to match types of learning with organizational settings.

2. Study learning and teaching styles.

3. Explore the possibilities of projects involving one-to-one instruction.

4. Design a comprehensive program of occupational or career education.

5. Free curriculum content and instructional procedures from the bonds of tradition by starting a school without any of the customary accouterments — without a physical building, instructional materials, schedules, or formal organization — and then see how teachers and pupils might redefine the learning process.

Programs Involving School-Community Cooperation

Several I[3] groups emphasized new projects designed to involve the community in the educational process. Specifically, these projects would:

1. Develop a totally new design for the problems of the inner city in which all appropriate agencies in the community would work

with the schools in an effort to deal with the total environment of the inner-city child.

2. Prepare materials explaining school programs for use by PTA's, schoolboards, etc.

3. Utilize community facilities (libraries, camps, museums, etc.) more creatively to meet learning needs of students.

4. Establish a program of working with parents virtually from the time their child is born to help them create an educationally stimulating home environment.

5. Develop a program of total family education, involving families, social agencies, and professional educators in studying topics such as child growth and development, adolescent psychology, and consumer education.

Miscellaneous Program Suggestions

Many of the recommendations received from the I³ groups do not fit into the preceding four categories. These ideas are listed below:

1. Train teachers in writing measurable behavioral objectives.

2. Examine the use of the computer to match student characteristics with teacher characteristics for making class assignments. A related idea suggested using computers to match teachers' characteristics with the needs of school districts and individual schools.

3. Develop programs to utilize school buildings and personnel more effectively throughout the calendar year.

4. Develop some type of program to attack the problems of racial isolation, dropouts, low achievement, and low self-concept.

5. Mount an attack on the traditional grading and reporting system by developing alternatives supported by research.

6. Study the contribution various psychological, health, and curriculum services can make to solving the problems of special education and other students.

7. Define the potential relationships between rural and large city schools and seek means of tying them more closely together.

8. Specify national goals for education and attempt to interpret these goals in such a way as to provide a guide for implementation of programs to meet them.

9. Provide for exchanges of students from different geographical, cultural, and economic settings.

10. Explore the contributions of home visitations by teachers.

11. Provide training in computer programing for selected school district and Title III personnel.

12. Place teachers on a twelve-month contract in which one month would be vacation, one month, in-service education, and ten months, work with children in the school.

13. Seek new evaluative measures in the affective domain of learning.

14. Define and analyze the roles of teachers, students, aides, and related personnel in various patterns of individualized instruction.

15. Establish a model child development center for children ages 3–12. Provide complete diagnostic services, teacher aides, and extensive materials for individualized instruction and give appropriate in-service training to the staff.

16. Explore ways to increase the holding power of the junior high school.

IDEAS FOR DISSEMINATION OF INNOVATIONS

Recommendations regarding dissemination tended to be similar among the various I[3] groups. Most of the suggestions were concerned with channels for communication and people who should be involved in providing and receiving information. A few recommendations were made, however, about the content of innovation dissemination:

1. Give information on failures and problems in innovative programs and on tactics used to resolve difficulties.

2. Summarize research findings and provide bibliographical references that relate to the content of Title III and I/D/E/A programs.

3. Include in reports of innovative programs a statement of objectives and the results in terms of the stated objectives as well as descriptive information.

4. Provide information about developments in the academic disciplines related to education.

Aside from these recommendations about content, the I³ groups were primarily concerned with what kind of dissemination channels should be used by whom and for whom. All of the major means of communication — printed material, meetings, individual and small group observations and discussions, and visual and audio media — were mentioned repeatedly. Specifically, groups recommended:

1. Provide much wider opportunity to observe innovative programs in action. Suggestions were made that this be accomplished: (a) by exchanging teachers, students, or administrators for sufficient periods of time to affect attitudes; (b) by arranging for visitors to be involved actively in the project as much as possible rather than being passive observers; and (c) by arranging internships for selected teachers to work for an extended period of time in a program related to needs in the teacher's own school area.

2. Organize demonstration centers that would provide operating examples of a range of new programs. Groups suggested that regional resource centers or "moon" schools be established for this purpose. Another possibility would be a consortium arrangement in which several schools within a local area would specialize in different types of innovative programs, thereby facilitating multiple observations within a small geographic region.

3. Use audio-visual media more extensively to explain innovative programs to educators and the public: commercial and ETV programs, slides, movies, tapes, and so forth.

4. Form a speakers bureau, perhaps coordinated by the U.S. Office of Education, to provide qualified people to speak to lay and professional groups about new programs. It was suggested that Title III project directors would be valuable resources for this purpose.

5. Organize workshops and seminars along geographic and/or content lines for teachers and administrators in innovative programs and for Title III personnel.

6. Encourage individual school districts to report on new programs at local, state, and national professional meetings.

7. Encourage regional educational laboratories and state departments of education to assume more responsibility for dissemination with emphasis not just on Title III programs but on all innovative programs, regardless of financial support.

8. Distribute regular printed summaries of funded Title III projects. These summaries should provide information that would permit school and PACE personnel to determine whether the program would be appropriate for their area.

9. Expand the ERIC system and train key personnel in its use.

10. Encourage horizontal dissemination of innovations within a school or school district.

11. Assign responsibility for dissemination of information to persons who have no vested interest in a project and will report the results objectively.

12. Give attention to the importance of getting information to people who do not seem interested in a particular innovative program (as a means of stimulating their interest).

13. Establish a model communication center.

14. Make efforts to utilize the information dissemination channels already established in professional organizations.

15. Organize teams composed of staff members from demonstration schools to conduct institutes.